PENGUIN BOOKS

THE UGLY CRY

Danielle Henderson is a TV writer (*Maniac, Dare Me, Harper House*), retired freelance writer, and a former editor for *Rookie*. She cohosts the film podcast *I Saw What You Did*, and a book based on her popular website, *Feminist Ryan Gosling*, was released by Running Press in August 2012. She has been published by *The New York Times*, *The Guardian*, *AFAR* magazine, *BuzzFeed*, and *The Cut*, among others. She likes to watch old episodes of *Doctor Who* when she is on deadline, one of her tattoos is based on the movie *Rocky*, and she will never stop using the Oxford comma. Danielle lives on a tiny farm in upstate New York.

Penguin Reading Group Discussion Guide

available online at

penguinrandomhouse.com

Praise for *The Ugly Cry*

Most Anticipated Book of the Summer with:
Good Morning America | *Time* | *USA Today* | *EW* |
Bustle | Amazon | *Bitch* | PureWow | *HelloGiggles* |
The AV Club | *Publishers Lunch* | Yahoo! Life | CBS

"I've struggled writing this blurb because hyperbole is unbelievable. Except the Grand Canyon really is astonishing and the universe does fill us with awe and Danielle Henderson's memoir, *The Ugly Cry*, is the funniest memoir I have ever read. It is also achingly sad. And powerfully redemptive. *The Ugly Cry* raises the bar on how hilarious and brave and weird and crazy and screamingly brilliant a memoir can be. Danielle Henderson has knocked it out of the park and into the stratosphere with this debut."

—Augusten Burroughs, #1 *New York Times* bestselling author of *Running with Scissors*

"Equal parts hilarious and heartbreaking . . . Her deeply honest writing is crisp, engaging, and full of life as it examines the complexity of identity, family, childhood, and independence."   —Associated Press

"Simultaneously heartbreaking and hilarious, Henderson dissects her unusual upbringing and her special relationship with her grandmother, offering a powerful examination of the many intersections between family and identity."   —*Time*

"The book scissored my heart to shreds. . . . *The Ugly Cry* is a vivid, voice-y, richly textured read."   —*The Washington Post*

"With wit and clarity, Danielle Henderson recounts her childhood growing up with her and grandmother—a ferocious and foul-mouthed woman who is not afraid to call it like it is. It is truly laugh-out-loud at points, which offsets the 'the ugly cry'—the screaming, the racism, the violence—of Henderson's experiences as a young Black woman finding her way in the world. An unforgettable and remarkable memoir that hits all the emotions of a life filled with love and heartache."

—*Business Insider*

"Danielle Henderson is a wonderful writer, and this clear-eyed look at her complex and flawed childhood did make me cry, as the title promises, but it also made me laugh—that is the beauty of a life well told. I look forward to recommending *The Ugly Cry* to memoir-lovers, to mall-lovers, to tough grandma-lovers, to tough-sister-lovers—to everyone, really." —Emma Straub, bestselling author of *All Adults Here*

"*The Ugly Cry* is funny and honest, disarming and bracing, like sharing a long meal with a new friend while she unspools the story of how she came to call her grandma the love of her life."

—Linda Holmes, bestselling author of *Evvie Drake Starts Over*

"Elder millennials in particular will find much to love in Henderson's descriptions of her late-Gen-X childhood." —*Bustle*

"Just as real life can so often be, Danielle Henderson's *The Ugly Cry* is both hysterical and heart-wrenching. The TV writer touchingly recounts how she was raised by a tough-as-nails grandmother in a mostly white neighborhood in Upstate New York." —*Real Simple*

"Can a book be hysterical and heartbreaking and smart all at the same time? *The Ugly Cry* can. It was painfully good and I loved it."

—Jenny Lawson, bestselling author of *Furiously Happy*

"[Henderson] renders her family with searing honesty and wit . . . [and] brings them to life with her indefatigable sense of humor, which is as quick and sharp as the violence she lived with as a child. . . . She opts for mirth over pathos, and the results are often shocking and funny simultaneously." —*BookPage* (starred review)

"The best memoirs . . . either have you wanting to go back to the beginning or will take you back to the beginning anyway, to live through

their vivid stories of childhood until you see something new about your own. I would submit Danielle Henderson's wry account of her childhood to this list. . . . Henderson achieves that rare memoir texture of detail and drama. . . . [It] is also a love letter to the unconventional and off-kilter family. Any reader would be so lucky to have Henderson's grandmother rip a Nintendo joystick out of their hands—because it's her turn."
—Sloane Crosley, *Departures Magazine*

"Henderson writes with an incredible amount of vulnerability, presenting her story with a clear-eyed compassion for her mother, grandmother, and, ultimately, herself. A redemptive memoir about a Black woman's victory over childhood abuse, racism, and mental illness."
—*Kirkus Reviews*

THE UGLY CRY

How I Became a Person
(Despite My Grandmother's
Horrible Advice)

Danielle Henderson

PENGUIN BOOKS

PENGUIN BOOKS
An imprint of Penguin Random House LLC
penguinrandomhouse.com

First published in the United States of America by Viking,
an imprint of Penguin Random House LLC, 2021
Published in Penguin Books 2022

ISBN 9780525559375 (paperback)

THE LIBRARY OF CONGRESS HAS CATALOGED THE HARDCOVER EDITION AS FOLLOWS:
Names: Henderson, Danielle, author.
Title: The ugly cry : a memoir / Danielle Henderson.
Description: [New York, New York] : Viking, [2021]
Identifiers: LCCN 2020043842 (print) | LCCN 2020043843 (ebook) |
ISBN 9780525559351 (hardcover) | ISBN 9780525559368 (ebook)
Subjects: LCSH: Henderson, Danielle. | African American women—New York
(State)—Biography. | Grandparents as parents—New York (State) | Women
television writers—United States—Biography. | New York (State)—Race relations.
Classification: LCC CT275.H5573 A3 2021 (print) |
LCC CT275.H5573 (ebook) | DDC 305.48/89607471092 [B]—dc23
LC record available at https://lccn.loc.gov/2020043842
LC ebook record available at https://lccn.loc.gov/2020043843

Printed in the United States of America
1   3   5   7   9   10   8   6   4   2

BOOK DESIGN BY LUCIA BERNARD

Some names and identifying characteristics have been changed
to protect the privacy of the individuals involved.

For Cory

All that we survived.

Don't think I forgot about you filling a water gun
with piss and shooting it at me just because
it didn't make it into this book, though.

Introduction

I 've never seen my grandmother bake a cookie, wear a shawl, give good advice, or hug a child unprompted. I have, however, heard her curse so intensely I swear she was making some of them up on the spot, watched her obsess over horror movies with an academic intensity, and listened to her frequent lectures about the reasons every woman should not only carry a knife at all times but also fully be prepared to use it: "A man wants to put his hands on you? Carry a little secret knife. Cut his throat. Ask questions later." Her favorite TV show is *The Walking Dead*; she likes to confidently conjure up strategies to survive the zombie apocalypse from her wheelchair, all of them involving rigged-up weaponry and fire. She knows she would triumph; after a lifelong cultural diet of *Creature from the Black Lagoon*, *Creepshow*, *Hostel*, and *Saw*, she has no problem thinking up ways to kill anything that moves.

And I was raised by her.

It wasn't planned that way. I had a mom once, and, along with my brother, we had a life together. When she left us at my grandparents' house for a weekend, none of us knew that she wouldn't be coming back. I certainly didn't know that I would spend the rest of my childhood with people who had already retired and thought their child-rearing days were over in the 1970s.

In the whiplash of trauma and figuring out how to adjust to this new life, dropped into the care of a foul-mouthed retiree, I realized it was up to me to figure out how to survive.

So I would take respite in the bathroom, the only sun-filled room in the house, where I could read in relative peace.

Every single person in my family yelled at me when they saw me carrying a book into the bathroom, which I did constantly. No matter what my business was in there, I usually sat on the toilet reading until my legs went numb. I shared a bedroom with Grandma, a twin bed under each window. It wasn't exactly my own space; she had already made me take down my Led Zeppelin poster, not wanting to look at "those sweaty white boys" on the few days a week she crawled up the steps instead of falling asleep on the couch. The bathroom was the only true privacy I had in the entire house.

"Dani, no—other people have to use the bathroom, you know," Grandma said, her lips pulling into a terse line as I walked through the living room.

"So then knock," I said, annoyed.

"Are you giving me lip, child? The library is right down the road! If you're in there for more than ten minutes, I will knock down that fucking door, little girl!" Grandma called after me.

When I wasn't letting my legs atrophy on the can while I finished chapter after chapter, I pulled back the shower curtain and climbed into the old bright blue clawfoot tub, using any towel hanging up behind the door as a pillow. I fell asleep in there once and woke up to Grandma standing over me. All of the skeleton key locks had long been painted over in this old house; none of the doors locked. It was easy to burst into any room if, like Grandma, you didn't value basic human privacy as a rule.

"Oh no, uh-uh, you are *not* allowed to sleep in the tub and hold this goddamn bathroom hostage when you have a perfectly good bed upstairs." She was pulling down her polyester, elastic-waist pants before I could even fully get the sleep out of my eyes, and farted loudly as she sat down on the toilet.

"Ew, Grandma!" I yelled, scrambling to stretch my long leg over the side and get out of the tub.

"Should've thought about that before you stayed in here for two hours," she said, gently unfurling some toilet paper. "You can sleep anywhere, but this is the only place I can shit."

THE
UGLY
CRY

1.

My mom and dad met in drum corps; I have no idea what instrument he played or even if he was any good. It would be weird if I did, since I don't even know what he looks like. His name was Carlton; he lived in Newburgh, about forty minutes away from Greenwood Lake, the small New York town where my mother grew up. They met at a parade. My grandmother didn't know that my mom had a boyfriend until he showed up to take her to her junior prom. There's a picture of them from that night, one of the only ones to survive my grandma's wrath; Mom was wearing a floor-length white dress with navy blue polka dots, afro picked out as wide as her shoulders. My dad was tall and handsome in his brown corduroy suit, the wide collar of his white button-down threatening to consume his shoulders. His afro was smaller, but the flash cube from the camera made the product in his hair glisten. In true seventies style, the photo is blurry and grainy; I can make out his features, but they don't add up to anything more than a generic face. They stood in front of my grandparents' fireplace for the photo, wide-eyed and slightly smiling.

My dad was a year older than my mom, and when he graduated from high school, his family moved to North Carolina. My grandmother chalked up their relationship to a high school romance and didn't really think of it again. She told Mom to get over it.

But my mom was not over it. Not in the least bit.

The summer after she graduated from high school, my mom got a job dressing up as Wile E. Coyote at Jungle Habitat, a Warner Bros. theme park over the Greenwood Lake border in West Milford, New Jersey. The park was filled to the brim with wild animals, and the main attraction seemed to be that you could watch them roam freely as you carefully cruised by in your car. As you can imagine, this was an idea with a terribly short shelf life; Jungle Habitat closed within a few years amid a litany of persistent scandals. One man was attacked by a lion shortly after the park opened; another woman was bitten by an elephant. Several of the animals got out and were found wandering around residential areas nearby. My mom's summer job was to dress up like a cartoon and welcome families to this pending horror show, probably taking bets with her coworkers about which of them would come out unscathed by the end of the workday.

At the end of the summer, after she had saved what she thought was enough money to survive, my mom packed a suitcase. She left it behind the shed in the backyard, which was rarely used, so she knew it would be safe. She hitched a ride to work with some friends and came home like everything was normal for the next few days. Then, one morning after she had confirmed plans with my dad—whom she had been in touch with all along—she grabbed her suitcase, acted as though she was leaving for work, and instead took a bus into New York City and another bus from the Port Authority down to North Carolina. At nineteen, she had decided that her life was her own, and she was going to use it to chase a man.

For decades after, my family would ask, "What happened to make her like this?" Mom had a run-of-the-mill, 2.1-kids, stay-at-home-mom kind of family. The kids wore matching outfits for the annual family photo at Sears and were surrounded by cousins, aunts, and uncles at summer barbecues. Grandma had been a different kind of parent to her than she was to me: when I complained about mildly blurry vision as a teenager, Grandma told me that my eyes were fine and "That's what you get for reading those fucking books all night when you should be asleep." When Mom needed glasses as a kid, Grandma actually got them for her. Running away was an abnormal event in such a normal childhood. Decades later, my grandma still asks herself what happened, a bubble of self-indictment quietly rising to the surface as she wonders out loud. "She was raised in the same house as your aunt and uncle . . . I just don't understand," she whispers, actively searching for a place to lay blame.

For the rest of their lives, they would never receive a satisfying answer.

My grandparents didn't know where my mom was for three

months. It was so well-orchestrated that when she disappeared, nobody suspected a thing—my grandparents, assuming she was dead on the side of the road somewhere, waited for the day they'd get a call telling them her remains had been found. Grandma started going gray. Granddad stopped talking.

"It probably took ten years off of all of our lives," my grandma said, recounting those months. "I was a wreck, your grandfather was a wreck, Rene and Bobby were so sad. Fucking selfish, in the end, you know? All that misery for a *penis*."

After contacting the police and filing a missing-persons report, my family sat and waited. It wasn't until my grandma got the idea to check the phone bill that they got any relief. "I saw all of these long-distance calls from around the time she went missing. I thought, 'Who the hell is she calling?' So I dialed the number, and she picked up," my grandma said. "Just as happy as a clam, like nothing had happened. I said, 'Robin, where the fuck are you?' She told me she was in North Carolina with Carlton." Grandma was getting annoyed retelling the story. "I don't know why, but I asked her, 'Are you pregnant?' She said yes. Just like that. I told her she better fucking stay there and slammed down the phone." My grandma seethes with anger when she tells this story, even now, almost fifty years later. "I didn't raise my children to be like that."

My older brother, Cory, was born in February 1976. My father was already cheating on my mom by then, and her life in North Carolina was bleak. She lived in a trailer with my dad on his family's property in a rural town; she couldn't afford the hospital bill after Cory was born, so she called her grandmother, Sweetie Pie, to wire her some money via Western Union so that she could take him home. He was all she had; she was so lonely she rarely put him down—but even when she held him, he cried mercilessly. She was exhausted.

A few months after Cory was born, my grandma got a letter from one of my mom's few friends in North Carolina. She said that Robin wasn't doing so well, but she seemed like she came from a nice family, and maybe she should go home. Again, Sweetie Pie wired her some money, and my mom and Cory took the long bus drive back to New York, almost two years after she escaped.

Granddad met my mom at the bus. He was introduced to his first grandchild on a platform in the Port Authority, surrounded by the noise and grime of New York City. He was so disturbed by the way my mom looked that he couldn't even speak; he hugged her but didn't say a word until the next day. She was wearing old men's clothes and was completely disheveled. Like no one was taking care of her, like she had stopped taking care of herself. Her appearance wasn't the only surprise my mom brought home with her; when my grandmother looked down, she saw my mom's belly protruding, like a grapefruit attached to straw. A small tidbit her friend had left out of her letter, but possibly the reason she wrote in the first place.

"Are you pregnant again?" my grandma asked.

My mom nodded.

———

My grandparents got creative to make space for three kids in their two-bedroom home. They took one of the bedrooms, my mom and aunt shared the other, and my uncle Bobby slept on the screened-in porch. Every single one of your neighbors would call Child Protective Services if you put a child on the porch these days, but this was the seventies, which was basically a lawless decade where children were concerned. Lawn Darts—a game where one child would stand in a Hula-Hoop placed on the ground and another child would aim for the hoop by launching oversize, spiky metal darts at them—hit its peak in this era for a reason: if your child was fed and moderately clothed, people turned a blind eye to your second-degree murder-adjacent shenanigans.

Bobby loved his space on the porch. He had blinds over the windows to cut down on the glare from the lake, as well as a large bookcase that gave him some privacy since the front door to the house was technically one of his walls. Birds used to land on the bushes outside his window, and he would cluck and chirp at them every morning. It was an idyllic room, if you didn't focus on the fact that it was the only way for every person in the family to get in and out of the house.

My aunt was not so lucky. After having her entire bedroom to herself for her last year of high school, she found herself rooming with her pregnant sister and a colicky one-year-old shortly before graduation. I'm not sure "cockblock" is the correct term; for the sake of my own sanity, I have to believe no one in that house ever had sex. But your pregnant, wayward sister returning like some kind of fucked-up prodigal mess would put a damper on anyone's lifestyle and make a lesser person lose their mind. Thankfully, my aunt has always been incredible and gracious, and she bonded with Cory immediately. Did anyone ever thank her for that? If someone showed up to my house *now*, pregnant and with an infant, I would break my own fingers typing into my phone as I tried to find them the nearest Airbnb.

When I was born, absolutely no one was prepared for me to arrive. Pregnancy wasn't at all like the checklist-heavy micromanagerial bonanza it is today, but you'd think *someone* would have at least been clocking contractions with mild interest in between popping cans of Tab and smoking cigarettes down to the filter. Mom and Grandma always breathlessly tell the story between bouts of laughter, amazed at my ability to enter the world despite their own ineptitude.

I imagine she had been uncomfortable all day, but for some reason, Mom didn't tell Grandma she was in labor. It was a little over a month before my due date, so it's possible she just thought she had gas. I've never been pregnant, but an extra helping of mashed potatoes is all I need to feel like there's a bowling ball resting on my spine for the duration of an evening, so I can forgive her. Grandma, true to form, told Mom to stop complaining and go back to bed. Grandma is a medical marvel; she had her motherly instincts surgically removed as soon as Bobby could talk, relieved that she was done nurturing now that her youngest child had an elementary understanding of communicative tools. Not the best person to have on your side if you're feeling a mild muscular cramp, let alone fully going into labor.

My mom couldn't sleep, of course, and finally told my grandma she was in labor. "I was so fucking mad because it was the middle of the night," my grandma says, still upset with me forty years later for waking her up. "They knocked me out when all of my kids were born—called it twilight sleep—so I was always coming to in the morning like a normal person. No one wants to meet a baby in the middle of the night."

Since neither of my grandparents ever learned to drive, they called one of my grandma's friends to help get my mom to the hospital. Darlene was white, but she was close enough to the family to get a Black nickname, so I've always known her as Nana Dar. She and my grandma first met at a school board meeting and just started talking one day after seeing each other around town. Like most small towns, Greenwood Lake was still a fairly prejudiced place to live—people scowled at my family, and many people wouldn't let their kids play with my mom, aunt, and uncle. But my grandma was bored and needed a friend, so she did her best to make friends. Nana Dar had a reddish bouffant hairdo and icy blue eyes that set off her olive skin. Like my grandmother, she smoked constantly; I can barely picture her without imagining a curl of smoke drifting up from her chin and dissipating in the air above her head. She was probably smoking when she showed up after midnight to take my mom and grandmother to the nearest hospital in Goshen. Nana Dar and Grandma were definitely chain-smoking the entire thirty-minute drive there. My mom was basically in the back seat crowning, and those two were up front, joking about how she better not give birth in the car, all while flicking clouds of ash on my fontanelle.

It wasn't long after my mom was admitted that I was born, on a balmy June morning at 5:00 a.m. in the middle of 1977. A nurse had knocked on the waiting-room window, and when Grandma and Nana Dar turned around, she had me in her arms. "She was holding you like a football, with your little chin in between her thumb and forefinger," my grandma says, stifling some laughter. "We couldn't figure out why it was so strange until we really looked at you, and goddammit, your eyes were *wide-open*. We couldn't believe it." She always takes time here to imitate my newborn head bobbing around, gazing out the window. "You were just dah, dah, dah, looking around, even though you couldn't see a damn thing. You weren't crying—just looking. It was the creepiest thing," she says, laughing. "But my god, you were beautiful. From the minute you came into this world, you wanted to see everything in it."

Moments later, my mom came cruising by on a stretcher, sitting up cross-legged and smiling. "That was fast!" she said. She was still wearing her socks.

I was a month early, but healthy and ready to go. When Mom and Grandma brought me home a few days later, everyone in the house was excited to meet me. Everyone except Cory.

Up until this point, Cory had been spoiled rotten. He was a cute baby with a teenage aunt and uncle, so someone was always around to play with and dote on him. He had two grandparents all to himself, and toys showed up without provocation. Cory brought a level of doll-like fun to the family; Aunt Rene and Uncle Bobby loved dressing him up in big sunglasses and wigs, while Grandma dragged him all over the house with her while she did household chores. He blended in seamlessly to the rhythm of the house, a tiny reminder of the ways families persist despite all the things left unsaid.

My mom and grandma had just gotten through the door; introductions were being made all over the place, and people were taking turns looking at me. Cory was nowhere to be found, but there was a steady thump coming from the bedroom. My mom called out to him, and he slowly walked into the living room, dragging a yellow plastic wiffleball bat behind him. As people cleared the path to my mom, Cory got closer to the mysterious blob in her arms. She bent over gently and said, "Cory, come meet your baby sister!"

Even now, Grandma can barely tell this part of the story without wheezing herself half to death. "Dani, he looked at you with those beady little hazel eyes, and then all of a sudden, *wham*!" she says, as she smacks her hands together. The thumping sound coming from the bedroom earlier must have been Cory taking some practice swings, because as soon as he saw me, he hit me in the face with that wiffleball bat as hard as he could.

"Oh, you started crying, he started crying, your mother started crying," my grandma says, rolling her eyes. "Everyone was crying but me. I couldn't stop laughing. That little bastard just popped you right in the face. Hilarious."

From the very beginning I was loved, even if I'm not sure I was ever wanted. Mom was welcomed home, but she was right back where she started, with more baggage than she had when she left. I was conceived on the run, the ballast that brought my mom back to everything she was trying to escape. One baby is manageable, but two babies, two babies when you are unmarried, when your boyfriend is actively cheating on you and seems to have no interest in the children you've created, two babies is too many to handle on your own. Of course Mom came home—a small part of her must have seen what was on the horizon, having just been through the late-night feedings and endless diaper changes with my brother, done mostly on her own. She came back, knowing that her bad decisions, her wildness, her recklessness would cover her in a permanent stain. She came back to restriction, to a mother who thought she knew better how to raise us, who made her feel small and stupid. She came back for us, knowing that Cory and I needed some of the family stability she took for granted, some of the structure she rebelled against so vehemently. Mom was home to stay—not by choice but by necessity, tamed only by circumstance. It was the first sacrifice she ever made for me.

2.

I n one of my earliest memories, I'm sitting on the floor of Grandma's living room, the fabric of her mustard yellow couch scratching against my neck while I clutched a McDonald's apple pie over my eyes with both hands in an effort to block out the world. The gray-green Zenith TV in the corner across the room provided the only light in the pitch-black living room. On the screen, Michael Myers walked through a building on fire. His slow, stumbling amble was only made scarier by the fact that the entire world around him was on fire. Was he alive or dead? I couldn't tell what was scarier: a living man walking through fire, or an indestructible ghost. I dropped the pie slightly when I heard the room spring to life with gasps and shouts of "Oh *hell* no," curiosity nudging me past my limits, as "Mr. Sandman" played over the credits.

I used to love sitting as close to that TV as possible on Saturday mornings, *Poltergeist*-style, right after Grandma turned off *Soul Train* and Mom started making her grocery list for the week in the lined Mead notepad with the red cover that was always next to the phone. I'd slowly wave my forearms close to the screen until I felt it—the fuzzy buzz of electricity still pulsing through the cathode that made the hairs on my arms stand up. It was a private game, a secret discovery. Grandma would sometimes come in to get the vacuum out of the closet and start her Saturday cleaning during my TV game; without looking, she'd toss out a quick "You're going to ruin your eyes sitting that close to the television, child," without even realizing it wasn't turned on. Sometimes she started vacuuming around me, running over the same spot a few times, trying to contain the ash from her cigarette as it made fresh piles in her wake.

But on this particular night, that television set became my worst enemy.

It was a regular occurrence for Mom and Grandma to invite friends over to hang out. Since Cory and I were still small and neither of them had a car, they were mostly trapped in the house with us all day. By the end of the week we were all on each other's nerves and at each other's throats, but a visit from a friend could help break up that tension.

For me, these nights were magical. It was easier to stay up past my bedtime when there were other adults in the house. They were so busy talking to one another that they didn't notice me sitting under the kitchen table playing with my Holly Hobbie doll or practicing with my Barrel of Monkeys. There was always so much laughter when other people were at Grandma's house; bottles of beer and booze that I'd never seen in the pantry would suddenly be piled up on the kitchen floor. If they were playing cards, a low, hazy cloud of cigarette smoke would float around their heads like a gauzy satellite. I wanted to know what was making them throw their heads back and howl like that, who they were talking about that made my grandma laugh so hard she threatened to pee her pants.

Occasionally someone would accidentally kick me under the kitchen table, and Mom would slide me out by my underarms and send me back to bed.

I remember being excited the night my grandma decided to scare the innocence out of me. There was always a moment when it was time for bed that Mom could waver—she could send us to bed before everyone started arriving, or, to our delight, she could choose to let us stay up. Cory and I hit peak wildness at bedtime, and it was difficult for Mom to control us—we always ran the risk of pushing her too far, to the point where she would turn out the lights, tell us to shut up, and close the door. Staying up late was an acquiescence for all of us—Cory and I made promises of calmness we could not keep, and Mom got to feel like she could get an hour or two of peace. The rush of adrenaline I used to get when someone told me I could stay up past my bedtime has since been replaced with the wave of euphoria I feel whenever I realize I can go to sleep before 9:00 p.m. But at the time, I was psyched. I imagine my mom was also psyched that there would be other people on hand to take care of us and give her a little bit of a break. If you ever wondered how difficult it is to be a single parent, just keep in mind that scarring your children for life is apparently preferable to reading *The Monster at the End of This Book* for the hundredth time in a row.

One of Mom's friends had brought over McDonald's apple pies for me and Cory; we curled up on the floor with our treats to enjoy whatever exciting movie we were about to watch with the adults.

The pie was lava-hot, so Mom told us to wait a little while until we ate it. Without the pie as a distraction, I was just straight-up watching a slasher flick at four years old. Every time someone was murdered, I felt the fuzzy-buzz feeling without being anywhere near the TV; I was electrified with fear. I would shout questions in an effort to get this feeling out of my body. "Who was that! Was that the killer!" I'd shout, while a cacophony of adults shushed me into silence. "Eat your apple pie," Mom said, her eyes in rapt attention on whatever was happening on the TV screen. I started taking the tiniest bites possible, not sure how long I'd have to make this comfort pie last.

The only thing I vividly remember about the movie is the end. Michael Myers walking through a room full of flames to try to attack Jamie Lee Curtis. Who knows how he got there or why he was doing it—I've blocked out the answers to these questions harder than the memory of the first time I told the boy I liked that I thought he was cute, and I refuse to watch the movie to this day. I only know that while everyone else laughed and shouted at the television in true Black family fashion, I let my apple pie drop to the ground, and I burst into tears as soon as Michael Myers's mask atop his slow-moving body appeared in the fire. The room got quiet for a second, and on the far end of the couch, my grandmother was looking at me. She doubled in half to lean over and look at my tiny, freckled, four-year-old face. "Are you *crying*?" she cackled incredulously.

I glanced up at my mom, sitting on the couch cross-legged just above me, the way she did when she pulled my thick, nappy hair into tight cornrow braids every Saturday. Her eyes were fixed on the TV, where we had just watched a deranged lunatic murder fifteen people in a neighborhood that looked strikingly similar to our own. Was I crying? "Ye-he-he-hessss!" I wailed. My grandma's sudden focus on my emotional state made me cry harder than I expected, and I let it all out in heaving sobs.

Without missing a beat, Grandma let out a huge laugh, which set off a tidal wave of laughter in the room. She quickly caught her breath and told me it was time for bed. "If you're going to cry, go cry in your room," my grandma said, taking a long drag from her cigarette and turning her attention back to the TV. "I don't want to miss what happens next."

Cory took little pity on my apple-pie-crumb-covered eyes and used the moment as a chance to cement his reputation as a tough kid. "I'm not scared," he said loudly, like a little snitch, from his position on the couch, where he was wedged between my grandma and Uncle Joe. I couldn't tell if he actually liked this movie or if he was just happy that I hated it so much. Everyone was already laughing, but this big pronouncement from such a tiny person made them all double over.

I was done with the whole scene—the laughing, Cory's bravado, and, most of all, Michael Myers. I used the couch for leverage and pushed myself up, then walked toward our bedroom to a chorus of "Awww, come back, Dani!" from some of the more sensitive people in the room. I walked slowly, wanting everyone to see the way my deep, sucking sobs made my whole body shake.

Nobody followed me.

I climbed into bed and pulled the covers over me, still wearing my overalls and a T-shirt. I cried myself to sleep to the sounds of everyone laughing and howling in the living room. By the time I woke up the next morning, I was in my soft, red onesie.

At least someone cared enough to put me in my pajamas.

———

We were living at my grandparents' house and sharing a room with my mom, the same room my aunt abandoned a year after my mom came back to New York with a newborn in tow. Aunt Rene had moved in with some friends in a small apartment in Middletown, New York, where she would soon start community college. I guess living with a couple of hapless nineteen-year-olds is far better than sharing a room with three people when two of those people are babies. The bedroom suddenly became all ours, a sort of studio apartment within my grandparents' house for our entire little family. Each of our beds was pushed against a different wall; when you walked into the room, Mom's bed was on the right, my bed was on the left, and Cory's bed was against the back wall. In that tight space, it didn't take me long to realize that Mom was a total pushover at bedtime. She tried to put us to bed at 7:00 p.m. each night, only to

spend the next two hours fighting us as Cory and I took turns jumping out of bed to complain about each other. We were two and
three; most of our complaints were just about the fact that the other
person existed. Mom would roll her eyes and ratchet up her voice
to shrill levels. The funniest was when she tried to persuade us.
"Don't you want to go to sleep so you can wake up tomorrow and
have Cap'n Crunch?" Keep your bribes, lady—when you're three
years old, tomorrow never comes. If we kept at it long enough,
Mom would eventually give up. "Stay up all night! Who cares! If
you're tired tomorrow, don't come crying to me!" We'd go wild
for a few minutes, blissfully unaware that the hammer was about
to drop.

Grandma had a different approach to our nighttime restlessness.
"If I see your little Black ass in that doorway after I tuck you in,
we're going to fight—you hear me?" I can only assume that most
three-year-olds get a bedtime story and a kiss on the cheek before
they drift off into sugarplum fairy dreams; my grandma would get
directly in our faces, squaring off with us nose-to-nose the way
boxers do at the beginning of a fight, and start leveling threats to
let us know she was not fucking around. Mom would try to inter-
ject. "C'mon, Ma, I got it." But Grandma was quick with a cutting
remark. "If you've 'got it,' why are they still awake?" Her house,
her rules, her stubbornness.

The only light in the house at bedtime was the pulsing glow
of the TV; Grandma would sit in her armchair and laugh her
Pillsbury Doughboy laugh, chain-smoking. I recognized Johnny
Carson's voice long before I ever saw his face. Every time Mom or
Grandma laughed, I felt like I was missing out on something. My

grandma laughs like Nelson Muntz, with a strong, punctuated "ha-HA!" on the end of every cackle, and my mom does more of an inward, high-pitched "HEEE!" that peters out as the breath leaves her body. Both of their laughs are infectious. Nothing made Grandma laugh harder than horror movies, though—watching people get killed in various ways always brought out her deepest guffaw. She considered horror movies training manuals for life; her response to people getting whacked was to laugh, shout to the TV about how stupid the characters were, and then tell them they deserved it. Even though I cowered under the covers at the sound of people screaming, the idea that there was a hilarious, secret part of the adult world that was unavailable to me made me furious. I tried angling my little body so that I could see into the living room, but most nights I just watched the shadows the TV made on Grandma and Granddad's bedroom door, drifting off to sleep in a haze of smoke.

Cory and I were rambunctious, and every night was a new chance to invite an ass-kicking. When you're small, there's nothing more terrifying than hearing the loud thunk and intentionally heavy footsteps of an angry adult coming your way. It's a portent of punishment, a signal that you'd pushed things too far. My grandma had perfected her stomp long before we were born, and she wielded it with precision. Once, in the middle of a fun game where we threw stuffed animals at each other and shrieked, Grandma stomped into the room and right up to Cory's face. I was frozen as she calmly told him through tight lips, "If you don't shut up and go to bed, I'm going to beat that little ass so hard you won't be able to sit for a week." I hadn't taken so much as a breath before she was in my face, the light from the hallway bouncing off her glasses. "You too—I will take you out to the backyard and leave you there." Her threats got less whimsical and more realistic the angrier we made her.

One night, Cory rolled out of bed to pee. Instead of scooting to the end of the bed and putting his feet down, he just rolled his little body right to the edge, thinking he would slide to the floor. Instead, he landed torso-first in the large, mint green Tupperware bowl filled with scalding water and Vicks VapoRub that Mom had put next to the bed to combat the drafty house and cure Cory's oncoming cold. In the seventies, it was perfectly normal for you to put a lava-hot bowl of water underneath your children's bed in the winter—you were lauded for your efforts at keeping them warm instead of being locked up immediately for putting them in the most obvious path of danger. I woke up when he screamed.

I don't remember much in the chaos of what happened next. My mom turned on the light and peeled Cory out of the bowl. Grandma stomped in and wanted to know what was the matter. Everyone started leveling blame—you shouldn't have put the water so close to the bed, you shouldn't have gotten out of bed, stop crying, call the ambulance. Cory's mouth was frozen open while fat tears slid down his face in a constant stream. He was in shock.

I didn't go to the hospital, but I don't remember who stayed behind with me as my mom and grandma wrapped Cory in a blanket and whisked him away. I cried—not because of the awful, encyclopedia-size red burn that I saw blazed across his stomach but because I was pretty sure Cory was never coming back. In my mind, after telling him one thousand times to stop getting out of bed, my mom finally set a booby trap, and he literally fell for it.

Cory did not die, but he was in excruciating pain for a while. He came home from the hospital, torso wrapped up like a mummy. The next few days were filled with his screams as he ran away from Mom every time she tried to change his bandage. He told me the other day that he can still remember the smell of the burn as if it just happened.

At bandage-changing times, I cried when Cory cried, convinced that Mom was still trying to kill him. Grandma leaned in the doorway of our bedroom, taking long drags from her Carlton 120's. "See," she said, squinting through the smoke to meet my eyes, "I told you to keep your little raggedy Black asses in bed. *Now* look." She used the cigarette to point to Cory and my mom, locked in a wrestling move as she tried to pin him down and simultaneously apply ointment to his wound. Grandma stood firm in her smugness, more impressed with how right she was than with how much we were all hurting.

The start of summer was marked not by a calendar but by the day Grandma finally decided to clean out the wading pool. For most of the year, it lived in the small shed in the backyard, propped against the lawn mower. I was afraid of that shed; it smelled too much like the ground after a thunderstorm and was pitch-black, even if you opened the door in the middle of the day. I dared myself to open it once; everything was covered in dust, and a daddy long-legs spider crawled onto my shoulder within seconds. I left the door open and ran toward the house screaming, swatting my shoulder the entire way. "Would you look at the hysterics?" Grandma said as I cried my way into the house. "It's just a damn spider!" Grandma never understood fear, especially if it was someone else's.

I cried every time Grandma had to go back there; I thought the shed would swallow her up and I'd never see her again. She'd already made me watch *Swamp Thing* at this point, so I knew what it looked like to be consumed by chemicals, fire, and water after watching the titular character run into a swamp and, presumably, die, only to be reborn as a mutant plant man. I kept a safe distance, but my morbid curiosity always got the better of me, so I hoisted myself up to the counter to watch from the kitchen window over the sink as Grandma marched around the house into the backyard. Whenever she was in the shed for more than ten seconds, I imagined her getting *Swamp Thing*'ed by an avalanche of dust, dirt, spiders, and centipedes. If she came back to life as a monster, I whispered to myself, I would not love her anymore, not even a little bit.

Instead of being turned into a grotesque, unlovable mutant, Grandma just came out of the shed cursing, swatting dust out of her hair, and rolling our Mickey Mouse wading pool to the side of the house with the hose. She cranked the flower-shaped spigot until drips of water started coming out of the green hose, bleached from a vibrant forest color to practically white after years of being in the sun. When she was done rinsing out the pool, I would run outside to hold the hose while she filled it up. I liked being in charge of something that I'd only ever seen adults do, and I liked it when my grandma said I was smart about something, even something as paltry as filling a wading pool.

The water was ice-cold, but Grandma always insisted it would warm up in the sun. "What if there are still spiders in here?" I asked nervously. Grandma looked at me over the top of her glasses, raised her eyebrows, and said, "If there are any fucking spiders in here, they're about to drown." But what about the bottom of the pool? There could still be spiders underneath. I would often look over the edge of the pool and see worms wriggling around where we had splashed out water, so I knew that this thing was a magnet for disgusting beasts that rose up from the depths of the earth. "I'm not going to sit here all goddamn day checking from here to kingdom come for spiders, child," she said, squinting to avoid the mist of the homemade spray nozzle she created by placing her thumb over the end of the hose. "If touching a spider kills you, well, I guess you were too delicate for this earth, and it was nice knowing you." My summers always started with a firm acknowledgment that I might die as a result of trying to enjoy them.

It turned out that the bat whack Cory gave me when I came home from the hospital wasn't just a funny story, but a portent of our whole relationship. Cory never forgave me for screwing up his sweet gig, and I never stopped narcing on him every time he tried to kill me. Cory's next window for murder appeared when I was learning how to walk. I was tottering around in my walker—a white plastic contraption with a wide tray and a little hammock seat with holes cut out for the legs—and Cory decided to jump into the three inches of space behind me. My grandma thought this was adorable and ran to get her camera. She snapped off a few shots before it registered that my face was turning red; Cory was shoving me against the tray with all his might, trying to push me out of the walker but accidentally succeeding in almost choking the life out of me. I cannot remember who swooped in to pick one or both of us up, but the fact that there is photo evidence of this moment says a lot about the people in charge of keeping me alive.

Now, a year or so later, after Cory had casually tried to drown me by holding his foot on my neck, I got a wading pool of my own, placed right next to his. This was the beginning of a decade-long standoff: Cory and I played *near* each other but not *with* each other. Over the years, our combativeness got more intense, until it fizzled out into something colder and more distant in our teens. It would be years into my twenties until I confided in him or felt like we had the kind of sibling relationship you see on TV. We were the polar opposite of each other from the minute we came into the world; our closeness had to be cultivated over time and after years of butting heads.

There's a photo of me standing in my pool, my tiny belly protruding over my tiny pink bikini, yelling at Cory while he played in *his* pool. According to my grandma, I was upset that he was splashing me. "You two couldn't be left alone for two minutes," she'd say with a laugh, "before you were trying to kill each other." Two pools should have been a great compromise; instead, I cried every day because he got the better pool, the one with the giant cartoon Mickey Mouse face on the bottom.

3.

A number of things factored into my mom's decision to put me in school early, not least among them my grandmother's insistence that "that little shit is getting too smart for her own good." I would be starting before my fifth birthday and had to be tested by my future kindergarten teacher to make sure I'd be ready to take on the rigorous work of naming colors and gluing construction paper hoops together to make a chain. My teacher, Mrs. Cross, was kind. She had soft blond hair permed into loose shoulder-length curls, and crinkles around her blue eyes that stayed on her face even when she wasn't smiling. At five years old, I was almost her full height, both of us meeting in the middle of her being impossibly tiny and my being freakishly tall.

The day I took the test, we left the sun-soaked classroom to finish business in the hall. The lights were off despite it being the middle of the day, and the dull green linoleum floor was a too-dark canvas for the shadows cast by the trees outside. Mrs. Cross and my mom stood near the classroom door; a different child may have skipped down the hall or found some chalk-based adventure in another classroom, but I planted myself next to Mom, eager to know if I'd be going to school or not.

"Danielle passed her test with flying colors!" Mrs. Cross smiled at Mom, then looked over to smile at me. "We'll see you in class soon." On the way home, I asked my mom to explain how colors could fly, again and again like a broken record. "It just means you're smart," Mom snapped, picking up the pace and trying to outrun any additional questions.

I loved being in school. The teachers smiled and were happy to see me, unlike the "What do you want?" reaction I got from Grandma every time I walked into a room. It quickly dawned on me that learning was something I could do on my own, something I didn't have to share with Cory. I liked asking questions and getting real answers instead of being told, "Child, I don't fucking know," which was Grandma's standard response. More than anything, I liked it when people told me I was smart, even if I wasn't quite sure exactly *how* I was smart—I just asked a lot of questions, then worked hard to figure out the answers on my own, like I'd always been told to do. But it seemed to matter a lot to Mrs. Cross that I'd been reading since I was three years old; Mom always read to us at night, and we went over the words together as I started to take an interest in reading on my own. Mrs. Cross noticed that I also had opinions about things, like why there wasn't really a crayon that matched my skin tone.

We also did fun things at school, like getting fingerprinted. The police were coming! To our class! Special! Taking time out of their busy jobs to visit us! Two police officers showed up one afternoon, resplendent in their uniforms and not yet a symbol of absolute terror. We were all sitting on the floor, our mouths open and tiny necks bent back in rapt attention. One officer talked to us while the other officer sat at the art table with a stack of postcard-size paper and prepared his kit. We ran through the basics, then lined up for our perp walk.

Our names were already written out on the cards and kept in alphabetical order, which should have been our first indication that Mrs. Cross was a damn snitch. The desk officer asked us our names, found our card, and made a big production out of placing our fingers on the ink pad, as if permanently taking away our ability to live off the grid was a special prize. He helped us roll each finger on the spots indicated on the card, and then—big finale—the thumbs, which were such an unruly part of the human design they had to be inked and rolled separately. We washed up at the art sink, drying our hands on the scratchy brown bark that passed for paper towels in the school system right up until I graduated high school.

As an adult, I realized the real reason we were getting inked was much darker: kidnapping was on the rise, and fingerprints probably helped them identify our tiny bodies.

I loved Mrs. Cross, even when she was fucking up royally.

We were coloring pictures of our families in kindergarten, practicing letters by writing each family member's title above their head. My family was easy to fit on the piece of construction paper—Mom, Grandma, Granddad, and Cory. The peach crayon was all wrong for their skin, but it was all that was on offer; Ryan Burke colored his family blue and had to start over again. I added everyone's names beneath their titles to fill the time. When Mrs. Cross came around to check my work, she praised me for knowing how to spell first names, but her next question confused me.

"What about your dad?"

I answered, without missing a beat, "I don't have a dad."

I may have smiled in deference the way I always did when I was talking to an adult, but talking about dads raised no emotion in me at all. I'd never met him, so I never missed him. As I continued to use the black crayon to draw the little swirls that looked most like Cory's hair, Mrs. Cross persisted.

"But, Danielle, everyone has a dad," she said gently.

"Not me," I said, without looking up from my drawing.

"Could you draw him anyway?"

"I don't know what he looks like."

"Maybe you can try to draw him, and then ask your mom how to spell his name."

Mrs. Cross had taught me how to hold a paintbrush and was the first person outside of my family to tell me I was smart without making it sound like an insult. I didn't want to disappoint her, but what was her fucking problem? All I could convincingly draw in the space of a father was a ghost. She had to have known it was entirely possible for someone to grow up without one or both parents—Charles Dickens had a cottage industry writing about orphans a century before I was even born.

Occasionally I would overhear my grandma talk about "that man" to my mother, always in harsh and villainous tones. "Why don't you ask *that man* for some money to take care of these kids?" Aside from that, he was never discussed.

Until Mrs. Cross's weird insistence that I acknowledge him, I had never really questioned the absence of my own father. I realized that other people had them—I knew that my granddad was my mom's father, that half of her everything came from a man who warmed her bottles on the stove, a man who pushed her on the swings, a man she could recognize on the street. I would hear other kids talking about their dads as disciplinarians, the looming threat their moms leveled at them in an effort to get them to behave. I didn't get it. My grandma was the scariest person I'd ever met, and I could not imagine any man having the ability to terrify me more than her.

"I have a granddad!" I said excitedly, trying to smooth over the situation.

"And what's his name?" she said expectantly.

"Jack. But sometimes my grandma calls him Robert? And some people call him Tiny," I said, having not yet grasped the concept of nicknames.

I drew a stick figure with a circle for the belly and wrote "Jack" on top of it, then took my anger and confusion home to my mom.

"Who is my dad?" We'd barely walked a block away from school, but it took traversing that length of the sidewalk for me to work up the courage to ask. When I did, it came out like an accusation instead of a question.

"Excuse me?" My mom was about to guide us across the street when my question stopped her in her tracks.

"We drew pictures of family today, and Mrs. Cross asked me to draw my dad, and I told her I didn't have a dad, and she said everyone has a dad," I said in that rapid-fire, little-kid way, afraid that all of my breath would leave my body before I could get the thought out of my head. "She told me to ask you my dad's name."

Mom, holding my hand, walked us across the street. "His name is Carlton," she said distractedly, keeping her eyes on the sidewalk.

This didn't help my confusion. She's known his name this whole time? What else did she know about him?

"How do you spell it?"

"C-a-r-l-t-o-n," she said.

"Where does he live?"

"North Carolina."

"Where's North Carolina?"

"Far away."

I could hear the tension rising in her voice, but I pressed my luck. "Why doesn't he live with us?"

Mom stopped walking, my hand jerking in hers as I was pulled to a stop next to her. She bent down quickly and pushed her face close to mine the way she did when she pulled me out of hiding in the clothing racks at Sears. "Dani, it doesn't matter, okay? And Mrs. Cross should mind her fucking business."

She stood up, and we started walking again, a little faster than before. We were silent the whole way home.

Getting to know kids around my age who were not Cory was re-
freshing. None of them tried to kill me, which was clutch. Making
friends turned out to be easy—you just found one thing you had
in common, like how much you loved the color green, and that was
it. Sometimes they talked about things I didn't understand, like their
dads or going to Disney World, but it wasn't hard to bring the conversation back to cartoons or who in the class could jump the farthest. I got along with all of the kids in my class. All except for
one: Lisa Weiringer.

I've changed her name because I truly don't know what happened to her after kindergarten. Despite our racially motivated ar-
gument, she could have become a prominent lawyer for the NAACP
for all I know. That's about as much grace as I'm willing to give her
now, forty years later.

Lisa was a bright-eyed, greasy-haired little fuck. We were in
kindergarten together; before the *incident*, I only remember her as
the first kid I ever saw to eat crayons like they were part of her
regular afternoon snack. Her crystal blue eyes and long black hair
offset the smears of dirt that constantly covered her face and clothes.
Her mouth always hung slightly open, like a kitchen cabinet with
a bad hinge, showcasing all of her wax-covered teeth. She shoved
classmates without provocation during the multiple times each day
when the class was forced to line up.

On the day it happened, Lisa burst out of the heavy double
doors first. Her parents were directly outside, sitting in their navy
blue Gremlin, a car that looked the way cars did when kids drew

them on construction paper—flat roof, long hood, and tires held
to the frame with Popsicle sticks. Two white painted stripes wrapped
around the windows and down toward the headlights. The comic
effect of this squashed, ugly car was only accentuated by the fact
that Lisa's parents were very, very big and smeared in dirt similar
to Lisa, as if the whole family rolled around in motor oil before
starting the day. Her father's glasses were so thick his eyes looked
like pinheads.

Cory and I usually hung out on the playground until Mom came
to get us. I had barely talked to Lisa and definitely didn't talk to
adults or strangers, so the fact that her parents were yelling at me
from the car as I walked to the playground caught my attention. I
couldn't understand at first; they were shouting a word that I had
never heard. "Hey, that's that nigger! You little nigger!" Lisa joined
in, pointing at me with her filthy little finger. "Nigger nigger nigger!" None of the other parents on the street said anything, even
though many turned their heads. Lisa went off to the playground,
and her parents sat in the car, glaring at me as I passed.

I immediately felt angry—not at the word, as I had no idea what
that word meant, but at the fact that they were all in on a joke I
didn't understand. I couldn't stand not knowing things. I turned
away and walked toward the playground, too, where Cory was
standing on a swing with his friends as they tried to impress one
another by seeing who could break their neck first.

"Cory!" I shouted, trying to make my tiny voice loud. "What
is a nigger?"

He kept pumping his legs until it looked like he was about to wrap the swing around the top bar. "I don't know! Ask Mom!" He pointed.

Mom was rounding the corner; she spotted us, too, and yelled at us from across the street. "Cory! Dani! Come on!" she said, waving her bony arm at us. Cory jumped off his swing directly onto the concrete, miraculously not breaking a single bone. I made sure to stop at the corner before crossing, checked for cars, and skipped over to her. "Mom!" I screamed, unable to control my frustration. "What is a nigger!"

Her eyes widened. "Where did you hear that word?" She was shocked, her voice an octave higher than usual. I got quiet. She had a look on her face that I'd never seen before, a mix of anger and surprise.

"Lisa Weiringer and her mom and her dad," I said, pointing at the blue car.

Mom's face clouded with rage; her pupils enlarged, and her smooth skin practically rippled under the surface as she twisted her mouth into a deep frown. She didn't tell me what it meant. Instead, her voice got the same high-pitched twinge it did when she was about to punish me or Cory. "They said that to you?"

I nodded, not sure if I had done something wrong or not. "Okay, come on," she said, lifting Cory up by the hand and grabbing mine on the way over. We were walking back in the direction of the school, in the opposite direction of home, trying to keep up with my mom's long-legged stride. Was I in trouble?

Without stopping, Mom looked down. She let go of my and Cory's hands and reached out for the first thing she saw—a giant fallen branch in the yard across the street from the school. This was definitely not a stick; it was heavy enough for her to need both hands to pick it up, and long enough that she had to drag it behind her like a cavewoman with a club. This was a weapon. Cory and I pumped our little legs in double time, trying to keep up. I was excited by the uncertainty of what could happen next.

We crossed the street, and Mom bypassed the playground entirely and went right for the Gremlin. Lisa's parents were still sitting inside while she played on the monkey bars. When we were about five feet away, Cory and I instinctively stopped and hung back a little as soon as Mom bent her face down right into the passenger-side window.

"Did you call my kid a nigger?" my mom yelled. Instead of waiting for an answer, she just lifted the branch over her head and swung it down, hard, on the hood of their car. It landed with a loud pop. Cory and I both backed up; she wasn't aiming for us, but she was swinging the branch so wildly we didn't want to get accidentally clipped.

At first, the Weiringers were stunned into silence. Who wouldn't be? My mom, a woman with the body of a stick insect, was circling the car, swinging a branch like a WWF wrestler. All of the kids on the playground seemed to move in slow motion; they stopped climbing and swinging and running, and the playground fell silent as all the kids watched my mom beat up a car.

"You want to see a nigger? I'll show you a nigger!" She scraped the branch off the Weiringers' hood, letting it bounce off the sidewalk once before picking it up again. This time, she swung the branch hard against the passenger-side door. Mrs. Weiringer flinched against the sound. The second swing seemed to shake Mr. Weiringer out of his silence. Soon he was yelling, my mom was yelling, and even Mrs. Weiringer joined in, all of them shouting some variation of the word "nigger."

"I'll show you a nigger!"

"Nigger!"

"Yeah, I said nigger!"

I had gone from never hearing the word until that day to hearing it about a hundred times in a row.

My mom dropped the branch and walked over and grabbed our hands. As we were walking home, she was still shouting over her shoulder at the Weiringers: "Mess with my kid again, I dare you. Yeah, you go ahead and try me."

Seeing my mom that visibly angry was shocking. But it was also exhilarating. My mom was sticking up for us. She was shouting for us, physically using her strength for us.

For me.

It was the coolest thing I'd ever seen.

4 ·

I was six when we moved away from my grandmother. Uncle Sy, Nana Dar's husband, purchased a small building in town; he opened a deli downstairs and rented one of the two upstairs apartments to Mom. Welfare paid for the apartment until Mom got a job working at Pendine Electronics, soldering switchboards. She didn't have any technological experience when it came to running computers, but she was nimble enough to weld the tiny pieces of the circuit boards together.

All of our furniture was cobbled together from stuff given to us by Grandma and Sweetie Pie—both of our beds, the couch Mom slept on in the living room, the big wooden entertainment center.

Mom must have loaded it in with some friends while we hung out with Grandma, because the day Cory and I were allowed to see it, the apartment was already furnished, already looked like ours. Small flickers of the familiar caught my eye as I cautiously crept around, like the small wooden end table in the living room; the brass handle on the drawer made a bright clink every time someone opened it as the metal gently swung back into place.

"And this is your bedroom!" Mom said with the uncharacteristic flourish of a magician. Cory ran in and jumped on Uncle Bobby's old daybed, pressed into the far corner near the windows facing the street, selfishly laying claim to the space like a cast member of *The Real World*. "Is this one mine?" he asked excitedly.

"Yup." Mom looked at me as I sat down on my twin bed, jutting out from the opposite wall, near the bedroom door. There was a small metal table between the beds with a lamp on it. "Is that a TV tray?" I said suspiciously.

"It's a table now. Cory, don't pull on that," Mom said, spying Cory tugging on the curtain tassel.

The bedroom was big, stretching across the width of the apartment and overlooking Jersey Avenue. Mom left us to explore for a few minutes. All of our toys were stacked at the opposite end of the room, near the rolltop desk Mom brought over from Grandma's house. The desk was too tall for either of us to use properly, but it was 1983—it's not like Cory and I were sitting at a desk by candlelight to do our homework like Laura Ingalls.

We absentmindedly played with our toys while Mom came back in and put a shiny sticker on one of the lower windowpanes. "What's that?" I asked.

"It's so that firemen can find you," Mom said, smoothing her palm over the windowpane. "This sticker lets them know there are kids in this room, so they should check here first."

We'd only lived there for five minutes and she'd already planted the idea in my head that we might burn alive in that room.

"What do we do if there is a fire?" I asked, frantic.

"Stop, drop, and roll," Cory said. He was crushing his army men together, not looking at us, and just repeating what his teacher had told him in class.

"Well, that only works in school," Mom said, looking around. "There's not going to be a fire. And if there is, just stand by those windows"—she pointed at the Tot Finder window—"until someone comes to get you."

I had a sudden twinge of loneliness. We lived on the dangerous second floor, without Grandma or Granddad or Uncle Bobby. The world felt smaller. I didn't know how we'd survive together, just the three of us.

———

I had nightmares for the first few weeks in the new apartment, and I told Grandma about them over breakfast at the All Seasons Diner.

"It starts over the doorway, and only I can see it," I said, jamming scrambled eggs into my mouth. We were sitting next to each other in the booth, our elbows touching. "And it's pink—"

"Don't talk with your mouth full, child." Grandma's cigarette hung out of the corner of her mouth while she stirred sugar into her orange coffee mug. Across from her, Patsy sat with her back against the padded booth, shaking salt onto her plate. Patsy was Grandma's partner in crime. She lived on Jersey Avenue, just like we did but farther down toward New Jersey, and would always come to pick up Grandma for bingo, breakfast, or shopping at the mall in Middletown. Her eyes were the color of a cornflower crayon, and, like Nana Dar, she wore her bright red hair piled high in a bouffant that was sprayed in place. Patsy had a soft voice and a raspy laugh, which we heard plenty of whenever she hung out with Grandma.

Grandma and Patsy picked us up once a week and took us to breakfast, and she came over to the apartment sometimes. I was always excited to see her and tell her about everything she missed now that we lived in different places. I swallowed the hot wad of egg without chewing just so that I could talk again.

"It's pink, and it oozes down from the doorway at the top. And then it gets bigger!" I held my hands apart for emphasis. Grandma looked down at me, squinting through the smoke.

"Grandma, can I have a pancake?" Across from me, Cory was kicking his legs against the back of the booth, hitting me every time his legs swung forward.

"Stop kicking me and let me tell my story!" I said through gritted teeth, leveling a solid kick to his shin. He frowned and kicked me back.

"You two! Cut the shit!" Grandma said, shaking her cigarette at us. Ash fell onto the table, dotting the greenish-gray swirls with black flecks.

"It's the Blob!" I said, exasperated. "The Blob is coming to get me, and it's in the doorway, and it's closest to my bed, so I'm going to get eaten first. And I dream it every night."

Grandma took a long drag, politely tilting her head toward the ceiling to blow out the smoke. "It's just a bad dream. The Blob isn't real. It's just a movie." She seemed bored and unwilling to acknowledge that she was the one who introduced me to this bad dream by making me watch *The Blob* with her, excitedly describing it as "a classic" and insisting I would love it. She stubbed out her cigarette in the ashtray on the table and turned to Patsy.

"She never showed up to bingo, ya know." Grandma always talked like she was exhaling, even when there wasn't a cigarette in sight.

"Who?" I asked, tucking a mouthful of food into my cheek.

"Mind your business, child."

I felt the sting of dismissal. All I ever wanted was to be part of the adult talk, the hunched-over seriousness and wild laughter and finishing each other's jokes. I perked up whenever I heard them mention a name that I knew, even if I didn't know what they were talking about. I tried to chime in, but the adults mostly laughed and shooed me away. My household nickname was Rona Barrett, like the then-popular gossip columnist.

Across from me, Cory tried to whisper while Grandma and Patsy talked. "The Blob is real, and it's gonna get you."

The nightmares eased as I got used to the new place. Our elementary school was two blocks away, and Mom could walk to work down the street.

Ever since we had moved, though, Mom seemed to have less

patience with us. At Grandma's, there were a lot of people around, so she could kind of spread out the job of raising two kids. At the apartment, Mom had to do everything. She didn't seem to like it very much, and it made her kind of bossy. She kept asking us to do stuff, to help out. Mom would lift the mattress as I learned how to quickly tuck the sheets under it. I didn't mind putting our toys away in the toybox or stacking the books on the desk; if Mom was vacuuming, it gave me enough time to sneak to a corner of the room and read until she caught me. The worst was helping in the kitchen, especially if I had to make the milk.

Of all the small injustices suffered as a welfare kid, powdered milk was surely the worst. Making milk was a whole production, and I hated every step of it. First, I had to climb on the counter and get the nondescript box from the shelf; it looked like a product from the Dharma Initiative, a white box with plain dark blue letters on the side. The box was bigger than my head and always threatened to topple me to the ground. I managed to slam it on the counter, crawl down, wrestle it over to the kitchen table, and kneel on a chair, where I would pour the powder contents into a plastic pitcher.

"Not so much, Dani," Mom would say while she was slicing cheese. Our cheese came in a brick that was the length of my arm and the width of my torso. The orangey-yellow made me think it could be American cheese, but the flavor was always a mix of something just north of cheese-ish, a pressed log of dairy fraud. The cling-wrap packaging had lines on it like a stick of butter, as if indicating that a normal serving size of cheese was a slice as thick as a magazine.

I stopped pouring, put the box down on the table, and lifted the pitcher to carry it over to the sink. There was an art to how to add the water: too fast and you'd just get foam, too slow and you'd get a thick paste that was impossible to mix. I learned to adjust it perfectly, feeling for the right setting after a few clicks of the cold water knob, and put the pitcher under the faucet. When it was close to the top, I'd teeter back to the table, climb back on the chair, and stir the whole slurry with a long wooden spoon.

To add to the injustice of having to make it, drinking powdered milk was hell on earth. It tasted like old batteries left to simmer in a puddle of hot rain. The chemistry of it didn't make sense to me, let alone the dubious nutritional content.

"This looks like water," I'd say, pouring the light gray liquid onto my Cap'n Crunch.

"And it tastes like doo-doo!" Cory would say.

"I want the milk like we had at Grandma's house."

"Well, I guess you just have to go out and get Grandma's house money!" Not all of Mom's comebacks made sense when she was stressed out or feeling judged by us. "Just finish your cereal!"

———

What I loved most about our new apartment was the bathroom. Ever since Cory had shaved off part of his eyebrow while no one was looking, Grandma never let us hang out in the bathroom at her house, but Mom let me sit on the toilet and talk while she was getting ready for the day. She was fascinating to me. Watching her was like seeing a peacock fan out its tail.

"What's that?" I'd ask, swinging my legs against the toilet.

Mom was plugging a small white box into the outlet by the light switch.

"It's a razor. Stop banging your legs."

I'd watch, enraptured, while she dragged the electric razor up and down on her armpits. "Why are you doing that?"

Mom was standing in front of the mirror, using the overhead light to gauge whether she'd missed any spots. "Because."

"Because why?" None of this made any sense to me.

"Because it's just what ladies do." It was a time when gender dynamics were often the period at the end of any sentence.

"Will I have to do it?"

"Yeah, one day."

My mom was usually in her bra and a pair of jeans when we were in the bathroom. Henderson women have—and I believe this is the clinical term—absolutely enormous tits. My mom's tits were always inching out of the top of her bra like a glass of water about to spill. Balanced on her tiny frame, they looked like a burden. One look at her and I'd decided that boobs were bad news, and I wanted nothing to do with them.

"Do I have to get boobies, too?"

Mom laughed. "Yes, Dani, one day you will get breasts."

"What are *breasts*?" I asked, disgusted.

Mom always asked me questions when we had our bathroom time. In our day-to-day life, she was kind of impatient, but she genuinely seemed interested in my answers in there. "What did you read in school yesterday?" she asked while dragging blue eye shadow across her lids. She always opened her mouth in a wide *O* when she put on eye shadow; I'd sit on the toilet and try to mimic the way her face moved, practicing for the day when I'd be old enough to wear makeup.

She always did her hair last. Mom had big, soft curls that she spritzed with something called "activator." I always asked her to spritz some on my hair. "You don't need it," she'd say. When Mom did my hair, she always gave me cornrows or tight braids. Watching her shake her hair around shaped my idea of freedom—there were no barrettes, no rubber bands, no bobby pins.

For her final display, Mom took out her teeth and brushed them. She had a big, beautiful smile, but her top teeth were full dentures. I don't know how she lost them or why she had them taken out. She'd reach into her mouth and pinch with her thumb and forefinger; after a few wiggles, she'd lower the tray of teeth right out of her mouth. I'd seen her do it a hundred times, but it was still thrilling to watch.

My baby teeth were falling out, so watching her clean her dentures made me feel like I just might never get teeth again. I think my mom was embarrassed, because she never wanted to answer questions about them. And I had a lot of questions.

"So will I get teeth after these fall out?" I'd already lost a tooth. I hated the taste of blood in my mouth, the loose feeling of it rattling around in my head.

"Yes, Dani."

"But if I don't, will you buy me some teeth like yours?"

"Goddammit, Dani, you're going to get your own teeth. Your adult teeth grow in after you lose the baby ones." Mom was busy scrubbing the soft, pink gummy part of her dentures. Her top lip looked slack above the space where her teeth usually filled out her face.

I was silent for a beat. "But—"

"Dani, go to the living room. Jesus *Christ*."

"I'll be quiet." Anything to stay in that space with her. I knew she didn't want to talk about her teeth, but I was enamored of the whole display. Getting sent away felt like I was being punished; I couldn't watch her swish the puffy brush around the blush and see precisely where on her face she put it. People stopped my mom on the street to comment on her skin, her makeup, her hair. No matter how many hours I spent with her in that bathroom, it all seemed completely unrelated to me, with my freckles, coarse hair, and stubby eyelashes; I don't resemble my mom at all. Mom made beauty seem like a magic trick I'd never learn. I think there was a part of me that was trying, in those moments, to know her deeply, deep enough so that I could one day bring to light any small part of me that was hers.

Cory and I were latchkey kids. Not in the traditional sense—we never locked the front door. I didn't have a key to any house I lived in throughout my childhood or teens. We didn't have anything in the apartment worth stealing, and if anything *was* missing, Greenwood Lake was so tiny that you would invariably see the thief using or wearing it. I was a latchkey kid in the eighties sense—your parents weren't home by the time you got out of school, so you had to fend for yourself for a few hours, and sometimes they just left you alone while they ran errands.

We lived on Jersey Avenue, and Pendine Electronics was about five houses down, right before the turn to Amanda Fennick's house and past Idonia Schermerhorn's house, where her dad parked his Corvette in the driveway. Jersey Avenue was a deathtrap from day one. The road hugs the twists and turns of the lake on one side, while the other side is littered with people backing out of the driveways of the homes they carved into the face of a tiny mountain that gave them the lake view they desired. Drunk, sweaty men were always hitching boats to trucks parked in the middle of the lane, or trying to load them into the lake from a jerry-rigged ramp at the marina. Pendine may have been close enough for Mom to walk there, but it was far enough along Jersey Avenue that I never wanted to, not even to walk to the pool.

Greenwood Lake had a history of people coming from the city to party all summer in the 1920s and 1930s, but those days had given way to something a little more woodsy and broken down, more *Creepshow* than *The Great Gatsby*. There were a few summer cottages behind Pendine that may have once been the center of summer night life, filled with sparkling headbands and beaded flapper dresses; by the 1980s, the owner had roughly chiseled an in-ground pool in the center where the unemployed men with belly bloat who lived in the cottages year-round floated around on inner tubes all day, blasting Van Halen from boom boxes tipped precariously close to the edge. It was a townie pool; someone had extended an open invitation to us at some point, and I'd frequently see kids walking on the gravelly dirt path on either side of the highway to get there, tubes and floaties hanging from sunburned shoulders. I could see from my bedroom window as cars narrowly avoided turning my classmates into roadkill. Mom wouldn't let us go because there was no lifeguard on duty. I didn't want to go because I didn't want my library books to get wet.

Mom usually got home around 5:00 p.m., and her single rule was that as long as we finished our homework, we could go outside to play after school. For Cory, play could mean anything from practicing handlebar flips on someone's BMX bike to finding a dead body in the woods and using it as a bike ramp. For me, it usually meant hanging out with Erin and Maureen, my only two friends in the neighborhood, until I was so irritated by the mucus-infused way Maureen pronounced "milk" (melk) and "bagel" (beg-el) that I went home to read something from my Scholastic book fair haul.

Occasionally, my after-school life intersected with Cory's, usually on a day when the social deviants he hung out with were being punished and had to go home directly after school instead of hammering nails through trees or taking turns knifing each other. During the summer we had to stay outside at all costs, but during the school year we were allowed to be in our apartment alone. My mom was tough, but she wasn't go-to-jail-for-letting-my-children-die-of-exposure tough. The indoor rules were simple: don't touch anything that wasn't in your book bag. Did you come home from school, grab a glass, pour yourself some juice, and camp out in front of the TV watching cartoons? Congratulations, Anne of Green Gables, your childhood was fucking rad. We weren't allowed to touch the glasses anymore after I broke the Hamburglar tumbler from our set of McDonald's fine china. We didn't have juice boxes because we were on welfare, and I would rather have chewed tinfoil than recreationally drink powdered milk.

We tried to watch TV once, turning it off as soon as we heard Mom's footsteps on the landing, but technology in the eighties was intent on destroying our flimsy excuses. "Were you watching TV?" Cory and I would give each other the knowing glance of liars everywhere and say, "No." Mom would then go over, touch the TV, and, feeling the warmth emanating from the screen, rip our story apart in three seconds flat. Disobeying her wasn't the worst offense—we were wasting electricity, and no parent in the country could abide using electricity for the intended purpose if they were not the ones flipping the switch. When Mom was home, you could fire up every light in the house, leave an empty blender running full speed, and overload every outlet until the fuses popped like fireworks. But children alone were unworthy of electricity, so I guess the expectation was we could spend our time weaving brooms out of hay and banging out candle holders on a tin press.

We had to make our own fun, so we invented Spiderweb City.

I say "we," but the first time we made Spiderweb City, it was completely Cory's idea. Breaking the rules was the only common denominator between us, siblings with a natural-born rivalry. Cory usually didn't spare me the time of day, but if I was willing to be his accomplice, there was an automatic truce. I was fine to sit in our room, making He-Man and Skeletor kiss on the parapets of Castle Grayskull until the sun went down, but Cory was antsy.

"Hey," he said. "Want to help me make Spiderweb City?"

It sounded dubious, but my big brother wanted to play with me, so I was all in. "Yeah! What is it?"

He ran into the living room with me hot on his heels and stopped short in front of my mom's yarn basket. Mom had always been an avid crocheter, and she made beautiful blankets. It wasn't uncommon to see her unwinding at the end of the day on the couch, quickly moving her needle all over the place and somehow producing a garment out of a single piece of yarn. It was magical to me. I had asked her to teach me and it took me a month to make a single crochet chain that was approximately forty-five feet long. I was very proud. Mom congratulated me, then ripped it out to finish the edge of a blanket.

"So we take some yarn," Cory instructed, pulling out a full skein. "And maybe some thread." He was making it up on the spot with the confidence of a boy whose only goal was chaos. "Then, we wind it around this," he said, making a knot around the post on the side of the entertainment center. "And bring it over here," he said as he ran the skein across the room to the doorknob on our bedroom, making another knot. "And we just keep doing it!"

I had to hand it to him: Spiderweb City sounded fucking brilliant.

I grabbed two skeins of yarn and put them under my armpits like footballs. We laughed as we took turns zigzagging across the room, tying yarn to everything that was nailed down and a few things that weren't, making a maze of string and discord until we couldn't move. "Let's do the kitchen!" I shouted like a frat boy with a fresh keg. The refrigerator door handle was proving to be a problem; it kept popping open whenever we tugged the yarn to tie it to the window latch.

This was the first time we'd really worked together on anything. It felt nice to put the simmering hatred aside for a minute, to drop my shoulders down from around my ears and have fun.

We had just decided to solve the refrigerator problem by propping a kitchen chair up against it when we heard the front door open.

Well, try to open. Mom couldn't get in and started to panic. "What the hell is going on in there? Cory? Dani?" Her face was poking through a crack about two inches wide, which was as far as the door would open. We army crawled to her through the web, giggling, and popped up in the few inches of space we'd accidentally left near the door. Looking behind me, I could see that the living room was a beautiful mess of brightly colored, waist-high yarn. This was so much better than that long piece of crochet chain I made. This was *art*.

"Open this fucking door!" Mom yelled. We pulled from the inside while she pushed, destroying some of our art in the process. The look on her face was enough to knock the smiles off of ours. Have you ever seen the gnashing, muscle-tight look of a lion protecting their cubs from predators? My mom looked like that lion, except we were the predators, and she was gearing up to protect her sanity.

"ARE YOU FUCKING KIDDING ME." There's nothing funnier than watching your mom try to beat your ass while immobilized by yards of yarn in every direction. She slammed through Spiderweb City like Godzilla, thrashing our experiment apart while we cowered behind the front door. "Cory did it!" I shouted. "No I didn't!" he shouted back, pushing me. Now all of us were shoving, waving, and screaming while the yarn maze held back our most intense attempts at landing a slap on someone, anyone.

"ONE OF YOU GO GET ME THE SCISSORS," Mom shouted. I resumed my belly crawl and scurried along the floor to the yarn basket that caused this destruction in the first place. If I helped her take down Spiderweb City, surely she would be more lenient with the punishment. I handed the scissors to Mom; she started cutting with wild inaccuracy, slicing any piece of yarn in her line of vision. "I have had it, you hear me? I'VE HAD IT!" I got out of the way of her chopping. She punctuated each form of punishment with every cut of the scissors. "You will NOT"— slice—"be allowed to play outside after school until I SAY"— slice—"so," she growled.

Our first punishment was to untie, unknot, and gather all of the string parts that now hung from every surface of the living room. The big wooden fork and giant, spade-shaped wicker fan on the living room wall that passed as art in most homes were the worst; I don't even know how Cory got the string that high. "Cory, will you help me get this?" I asked quietly.

Cory looked at me. "Do it yourself, idiot," he whispered.

I threw the scissors at him. They landed a few inches away from his toes. Mom saw the whole thing, picked me up by my wrist, and spanked me as hard as she could on my ass before sending me to bed. "You could have really hurt him!" Mom screamed, the irony lost on her. Cory stifled a laugh through the whole thing.

I had enjoyed our fleeting truce. But as I looked at him through tears on my way to the bedroom, something about hating Cory with all my might just felt right.

One morning Mom was already at work, and Grandma had come over to help us get ready for school when she dropped the news that she and Granddad were moving over the mountain to Warwick. They had found a duplex on a dead-end street near the cable company right in the middle of town, which would be convenient since neither of them knew how to drive. They could walk to the Grand Union for groceries. It was the perfect place for their retirement. The only thing that registered for me was that they were moving away.

When Grandma helped us get ready for school in the winter, we always got dressed in the kitchen. Our apartment had working heat, but Grandma insisted that getting dressed in front of the stove would keep us from getting colds. As soon as she came in, coat still on, she'd crank the oven to four hundred degrees and turn on the radio. After she made a cup of coffee she'd wake us up and march us to the bathroom right off the kitchen for our sponge bath, which consisted of us using a washcloth and a bar of Ivory soap to wash our face and body. While Cory and I were busy washing and fighting over the soap, she'd open the oven door and fill the kitchen with heat, then go get our clothes and set them on the kitchen table, sipping coffee until we ran out in our undershirts and underwear.

"What's retirement?" I asked. Grandma was pulling a shirt over Cory's head, and I was staring at the coils in the wide-open oven.

"Dani, don't touch that. Retirement is when you stop working," she said, wrestling Cory into a pair of jeans. "Put your LEG IN THERE, child, and stop messing around."

"But you don't have a job." Grandma had worked as a babysitter in the past, but she had been a stay-at-home mom since her kids were born. She had time to get us ready in the morning, but that didn't mean she needed to take shit from a little kid about her life choices in the process. She gave me a pursed-lip look but didn't answer. I was wondering if there was anything I could throw into the oven just to watch it burn as the heat turned my cheeks a rosy red. I crouched down closer, mooning the open oven, feeling the heat wrap around my butt and pass over my back. Would my braids burn if I got too close? Could I throw a barrette in there?

"Get away from the goddamn oven, Dani," Grandma said, reading my mind. She was trying to loop Cory's elastic belt through his jeans but gave up. "Here," she said to him, "you finish this before your sister goes up like a Roman candle. Dani, get over here."

I bounced over, my bare feet slapping the warm linoleum. "You don't have to have a job to retire; you just have to get old." Grandma was buttoning my shirt. She always buttoned them right to the top, so that I felt like I was being choked by a tuberculosis-ridden Victorian mistress all day.

"How will we see you?" I asked.

"You're seeing me right now."

"But what if we want to see you and now you live far away?"

"Dani, it's a fifteen-minute ride over the mountain. I'll take a cab." She softened a little, cupping my face in her hands. "If you want to see me, just call me." She planted a kiss on my forehead.

I knew how to dial the phone and had already memorized two phone numbers: Grandma's and the Mr. Yuk poison control hotline, thanks to the green-and-black sticker on the handle. I was soothed for the time being.

"Cory, turn that off," she said, giving a head nod to the radio.

"No!" we both protested immediately. David Lee Roth was singing "I Ain't Got Nobody," and our favorite part was coming up.

"Is this that white man that jumps around all over the place?" Usually she would have to be more specific, but I'd already seen a few hours of MTV over at Erin's house and knew she was talking about Van Halen's song "Jump," the pump-up anthem of every kid we knew, the soundtrack to every hyperactive moment, the permission we needed to throw ourselves around the room and leap off of anything in sight.

"Shhhh, it's coming up!" I said, tracking the song. Memorizing lyrics was one thing Cory and I would do together without wanting to murder each other. We sat at the playground one day trying to memorize the Vincent Price part of "Thriller"; when we nailed it, he was so excited that he jumped off a swing.

Now, in our overheated kitchen, with the radio blaring and Grandma frowning, we tipped our heads back in unison and sang along with the white man who couldn't stop jumping.

"HUMMILY BABILY ZIBBILY BOOBILY HUMMILY BABILY ZIBBILY BOP!"

Cory and I immediately fell out laughing.

"You kids are idiots," she said, laughing with us. "Come on—turn off the stove. Let's get to school."

It was during one of these walks to school that I decided to tell my grandmother about a major decision I had made.

"Grandma. I'm never going to college, and I'm never having babies."

She stopped dead in her tracks.

"What on earth would make you say that?" She was trying to stifle her laughter but wasn't doing a very good job. I don't blame her—it's not every day a seven-year-old prophetically announces their future plans with such an adamant approach.

"College is like jail. And babies are gross."

We started walking again. Cory had already zoomed ahead of us to meet his friends on the playground before school started, so I had Grandma's full attention.

"Dani, what makes you think college is like jail? You don't know anything about it."

"Aunt Rene went to college. She moved away and wasn't allowed to come home anymore."

Grandma was in full Pillsbury Doughboy laugh now. "What the fuck are you talking about?" she said, wiping away tears. "Rene wanted to move! And of course she can come home!"

"No. It's like jail. Jail and school."

"Okay, child. And what about babies?" Grandma was humoring me. I started to get angry—this was a serious discussion, and I demanded to be heard.

"No one likes babies. They just poop and pee and scream."

Grandma stopped again so that she could hold her stomach while she doubled over laughing. When she was able to regain her composure, she tried to ask me questions with a straight face.

"I loved having babies. One day you're going to want a family, too."

"I already have a family," I said. "And Cory is a stupid doo-doo head."

No one in the eighties was particularly adept at discussing bodies or sex, but that hadn't stopped my mom from sitting me and Cory down a few weeks earlier to tell us about reproduction. We had found her tampons in the bathroom, pulled a couple out, and started throwing them around the living room, so she thought it was time.

I have to give it to her—it was a novel approach. First, she explained it clinically, that Cory had a penis and I had a vagina. We were like, duh, catch up, Mom, we've been taking baths together for years now, so that was pretty obvious. Then she explained that when a man and woman love each other, they have sex, which is putting the penis into the vagina. We were both disgusted and took turns sticking out our tongues and making fake puke sounds while Mom tried to get our attention again.

The real kicker came when she described periods and childbirth using imagery she knew we would understand: Six Flags Great Adventure. "Women have eggs, and they're like the people in the roller-coaster car," she said, nary a smile on her face. "And the roller-coaster tracks are the tubes they go through. So the eggs are flushed out every month, like the roller coaster going down the track— you know, the one with the splash at the bottom?—and that's a period, and that's why I have tampons. To stop the splash. Except the splash is blood." She paused. "Tampons are not toys."

I didn't want to know any of this—about my body, or Cory's body. This sounded like the plot to the horror movies I was already so well-versed in, thanks to my grandmother. But she wasn't done.

"If the man's sperm and the woman's egg come together, they make a baby. And then you don't have the splash while the baby is growing inside your belly," she said, pointing to me.

"Wait—I have to grow the baby?" I asked, incredulous. "In here?" I said, pointing to my belly button.

"Yes."

"No way, José. I'm not doing that."

"Everyone does it, Dani."

"Not Cory! Cory doesn't do it." The burgeoning coals of what would become my feminist fire were sparking to life as I pointed at my brother, innocently sitting next to me. "How do they get that baby out of there?"

"It comes out through your vagina."

It was impossible for either of us to know it at the time, but those six words changed my life. At seven years old, I had barely become acquainted with my vagina before I knew I had to protect it at all costs.

I relayed this information to Grandma as we approached the school.

"Babies come out through your stomach and vagina," I said emphatically. "I am not doing that."

Exhausted from laughing, Grandma finally gave in. "Okay, child, whatever you want. Have a good day at school," she said, kissing my forehead before I ran inside.

5·

The fact that I don't believe in God certainly didn't stop me from lying to his employees for a few years.

We're not a religious family in the traditional sense. I've only seen my family genuflect when boxes of Entenmann's pastries are on sale two-for-one at the Grand Union, and 60 percent of us were born so far out of wedlock our birth certificates list "who cares" in the space where you indicate the father's name. Christmas was a time best spent ripping pages out of the three-hundred-pound Sears catalog and begging for thousands of toys that would never make their way under the tree; Easter was the season for eating tie-dyed egg salad for a week straight to help revive you from the self-administered, candy-induced diabetic shock of your overflowing Easter baskets. Who rose from the *what*? Pass the M&M's.

I was baptized in the Catholic Church a few months after I was born and didn't step foot in a church again for seven years. They were big on protecting the soul, but there wasn't much God in my life following my baptism, aside from the casual way every adult in my family took the Lord's name in vain every ten seconds. Like all Black families raised in the jive-talking seventies and politically oppressive eighties, "goddamn" was the most widely used descriptor of all things animal, vegetable, or mineral. Though sometimes used aggressively, it was primarily a gentle way to indicate the world-weariness and overall exhaustion cultivated deep in the bones of all middle-aged Black folks. It filled a space, and your job was to figure out how to read between the lines of what each "goddamn" actually meant. "I said pass the goddamn salt" meant you were tired after a long day, certainly too tired to repeat yourself. "Do you know where my goddamn gloves are?" was code for "Which one of you moved my stuff after I expressly told you not to move my stuff?" The rapid-fire, multiple wielding of "goddamn" was a threat-level-red situation, a clear sign that you had just pushed someone to the limits of their sanity. It wasn't unusual for my grandma to condemn me straight to hell for not letting her *goddamn* play the *goddamn* Nintendo she *goddamn* bought for these little *goddamn* motherfuckers. It was her expletive-laden form of praying that someone, *anyone*, would give her the strength to keep from murdering me for trying to level up on *The Legend of Zelda* when it was clearly her turn. When she dies, I will make sure her tombstone simply reads:

GODDAMMIT, I TOLD YOU KIDS TO LEAVE ME ALONE

We were a baptized bunch, but regular church attendance was never on the menu. My grandmother spent her Sunday afternoons chain-smoking foot-long Carlton 120's and yelling at the Jets, Giants, Mets, or Knicks to throw, kick, punt, or pass whichever ball was in play. My grandfather open-mouth snored loudly in the armchair next to her, shifting slightly every time she yelled, "Shut up, Jack," his snoring apparently more irritating than her exasperated wails. He usually went back to sleep quickly, patiently waiting for her to calm down or just give up so he could change the channel to WPIX and watch one of the Westerns that aired all day. If Sunday was the Lord's day, we were only taught to pray to the gods of the split-finger fastball and John Wayne.

Thinking I'd miraculously skipped out on all manner of religious instruction, you can imagine my surprise when out of the blue my mother informed me that I had to attend church school in preparation for my communion. "Don't forget to go with Erin and Mrs. Garrett after school on Tuesday," she said nonchalantly one day as she mixed a jug of powdered milk at the kitchen counter. "You're going to church school."

There was little to protest since I had no idea what she was talking about, but I gathered up all of my seven-year-old might to rail against the idea of extra instruction. "Why do I have to go to school *after* I go to school?!" I complained, tiny pigtail braids slapping against my ears. I was a decent student, but my afternoons were already filled with chasing Tommy Garrett around the swings and punching him in the solar plexus for calling me a tomboy.

"You're going to church school."

"Why?"

"Because I said so."

"Why?"

"Because I need a goddamn break," she said, dropping the wooden spoon in the container, "and your goddamn grandmother is making me do it, so I'm making you goddamn do it."

Having heard the multiple Henderson "goddamn"s, I knew it was useless to fight her.

It was a short walk to the squat, stone church that housed the answers to life, the universe, and why my family thought I needed to be indoctrinated in a dominant religion that had wreaked globally destructive havoc on brown people who looked just like me for centuries. Mrs. Garrett walked a group of us to the church the first week, but after that we were expected to get there on our own, even though six-year-old Adam Walsh had been kidnapped and murdered three years earlier and concerns about child abduction were on the rise.

Throughout the eighties, kidnapping was deployed as an empty threat by overworked, exhausted parents who wanted to keep us close enough to elude Child Protective Services but far enough away to not ever have to see, hear, or smell anything we were playing with. "Oh, you want to run off and play on Elm Street without telling me where you're going? That's the fast-track to getting kidnapped!" my mom said, looking very refreshed after the three-hour nap my absence afforded her. These days, children are embedded with GPS systems in utero, but in the 1980s, we had a low-rent solution to potential child snatching: the secret password. Every parent in my neighborhood used this method, teaching us to ask strangers for the secret password before they tried to take us anywhere. The built-in trick was that the potential kidnapper wouldn't know the password, so you could then scream or run away. It's an oddly polite reaction to a serious attempted crime, and, to my knowledge, it never worked once. Can you imagine?

"Get in the van."

"Pardon me, sir, but do you happen to know my secret password?"

"Uhhhh . . . pizza."

"'Twas peanut butter and jelly, my good man! Now unhand me and I'll be on my merry way."

The secret password gave some parents enough ammunition to appear capable and concerned while still forcing us to stay out of their way as much as possible. And, in a brilliant stroke of the prescient victim-blaming mentality that would become de rigueur thirty years later, it also made any potential kidnappings entirely our own fault.

"Didn't you used to have *three* children?"

"Well, Suzanne didn't use the secret password when a stranger tried to force her into their car, so she had to get snatched. Dem's da breaks! Let's strap on some shoulder pads, stick some Lee Press-On talons on our fingernails, and get a shrimp cocktail."

We toddled off to church school, with only God and a few snack-based phrases to protect us.

Holy Rosary was a small stone church on Windermere Avenue. It reminded me of the type of house you would see in a fairy tale, an unassuming place where the townspeople lived. The neighborhood was quiet; if you kept walking down the street, you would hit the top of the lake.

The schoolroom was just a room in the basement, filled with small plastic chairs lined up in rows. The teacher, a dowdy woman who was likely a volunteer, made us all sit down. We instinctively knew to be quiet, since "school" was in the title, but, as a kid who never went to church, I had no idea what else was about to happen.

After the teacher handed out the pink catechism books, we were invited to go to the wooden booth to confess to the priest. I sat in the dark box and was startled when the small rectangular screen slid open next to my elbow. "Hello, my child." The priest asked me to call him Father, a word that sounded unfamiliar in my mouth, and confess my sins. As a book-obsessed seven-year-old I had absolutely no idea what he was talking about, so I did the thing that came naturally: I lied my ass off.

"Um, I broke my mom's favorite mug," I said confidently.

"And how did that make you feel?"

"Uhhh . . . bad?"

"Say ten Our Fathers and three Hail Marys."

Well, that was easy.

Like serial killers and three of the worst men I ever dated, I never really had a grasp on what I was supposed to feel sorry about. Week after week, I filled the confessional with lies. I yelled at my teacher. I stole my best friend's favorite toy. I kicked a dog. I punched my brother in the nuts. No one ever caught on, verified my story, or gave me more of a punishment than walking to a pew to chant a few quick Our Fathers on a plastic rosary. It slowly dawned on me: if I could lie and be quickly forgiven, there was nothing to stop me from actually doing some of the stuff I was making up. Catholicism flipped a switch and turned me on to a life of crime.

First, I stole a pack of purple jelly bracelets from Hanley's Lotto, which doubled as a five-and-dime. Purple was my favorite color, and the bracelets were the most prominent status symbol of the first-grade set. Instead of buying them one at a time, I took the whole package and stacked them halfway up my arm. Within three weeks, I had a rainbow of stolen goods that I cleverly looped into a jump rope. I said a few Hail Marys and slept soundly.

My neighbor Kurt always teased me for being tall; after I learned that I could be forgiven for anything in confession, I started beating him up with gusto.

My days of lying and thieving lasted until my first communion. I had a loose grasp on what I needed to do in order to be communed aside from an agonizing day spent in Sears buying a miniature wedding dress replete with a tiny child-bride veil, but the fact that my whole family was coming seemed like a big deal. My great-grandmother, Sweetie Pie, came up from New York City wearing her finest daytime turban, her light skin offset by a pair of giant dark sunglasses. She had a deep, croaking voice and spoke in a slow, quiet way that made her seem like the most glamorous woman I'd ever meet. It's hard to imagine her sitting on a graffiti-filled subway and enduring a nauseating two-hour-long bus ride to get there when she clearly should have arrived in a crystal carriage powered by unicorns. Sweetie Pie and Grandma talked on the phone almost every day, but she only came to see us a few times a year. She always carried a camera with her, the kind with the long flash cube attached to the top, and would read books with me for as long as I wanted. When the rest of the city family visited once a year, she drove up with them but hung out with us. While the other adults were in the kitchen cooking, playing cards, and drinking beer, Sweetie Pie was outside, listening intently to our instructions about which rock was a base for the game we just made up. She took pictures of us while we ran around; without her there to document it, the happier part of my childhood would be an unattainable memory.

My mom curled her hair into a Farrah Fawcett bouffant, covered her entire eyelids up to the brows in turquoise eye shadow, and wore a maroon, tapered jumpsuit under a short white blazer; she looked like a Rainbow Brite doll about to turn tricks. My grandmother was busy being choked by a shirt with so many ruffles I thought her skin would be permanently marked with undulating waves, but her Jheri curl was spritzed to high heaven, shining brighter than the safety reflectors on my bike wheels. My grandfather wore the same thing he always wore—a thin plaid shirt with the top two buttons undone and a pair of jeans—but he deigned to put on a pair of shiny black shoes. My brother was also part of this communion and wore a tiny black suit with a white shirt and tie. There's a picture of all of us standing in front of the church; without context, it looks like a hooker, her parents, and their madame are happier than ever to marry their youngest children to each other before they hand them over to the pope.

The ceremony was long and forgettable; legions of children marched up to the podium one by one and listened to the priest mumble something in Latin before he shoved a dry Styrofoam disc in our mouths and made the sign of the cross over his elaborate robe. The body of Christ tasted like construction paper and felt like a giant, doughy penny as it dissolved on my tongue.

When it was over, I asked my grandmother excitedly what was next. I was already planning my next attack on Kurt and wanted to know when I could come back to church to be forgiven for it.

"What do you mean, 'what's next'?" my grandmother said.

"When do I come back to confession?" I said.

My grandmother looked down at me, her mouth terse and one eyebrow raised. "Child, we're not coming back here! We don't have time to get your ass to church every week." She walked away briskly, barking at everyone to pile into the cab so we could go home in time for her to catch the next game.

My communion marked the beginning of my soul's salvation and the end of stealing. It was a relief—I had a hard time believing in God, and I was running out of stuff to make up in confession.

Even though I didn't have to go back to church anymore, I was still learning how to keep on the right side of good versus bad. One day, while grocery shopping with Mom in Grand Union, I looked down and saw a roll of bills on the ground held together with a thin rubber band around the middle. I picked it up; it was heavy in my hand and the size of a roll of toilet paper. The outside bill was a twenty; even if the rest of the roll was singles, it was the most money I'd ever held in my life. I ran over to Mom.

"Look what I found!" I was excited. Like any seven-year-old, I was well aware of the Finders Keepers rule—anything you found that didn't directly belong to you was now yours. It was a biased and rather Republican approach to material goods, but now that the law was working in my favor, it felt just.

"Give me that!" Mom snatched the roll out of my hand. "Where did you get this?"

I pointed to the ground. "There. It was on the ground!" I was already calculating how many video game quarters this would yield and how much I could rub it in Tommy's face that I was now at the top of the *Pole Position* scoreboard.

"Come on," Mom said, abandoning our cart.

We walked to the front corner of the store. The manager sat on a raised, dais-like platform in an office-size box. His gray vest strained at his midsection, the buttons threatening to pop at such velocity they would surely take out someone's eye. He peeked out at us through the window at the counter. "May I help you?"

"My daughter found this in an aisle," Mom said, handing up my roll of bills through the window.

When the betrayal of the situation hit me, I yelled, "That's mine! I found it!" I stomped my foot and screwed my face up, pointing an accusatory finger at Mom. "Finders keepers!" Mom was twenty-eight, so it's possible she had forgotten the rules all children lived by, but I was happy to remind her.

Mom grabbed my wrist, pushed my arm down to my side, and pointed her finger in my face as she bent down to meet my gaze. "It is *not* yours. Someone dropped this, and we don't keep things that don't belong to us. That's stealing. *We don't steal.*" Her big brown eyes were wide with anger.

"If you could maybe put it in an envelope or something? I'm sure someone will come looking for it," Mom said to the manager. He took off the rubber band and flattened out the bills; they were all twenties. "Sure," he said, reaching for an envelope and stuffing the money inside. "Thank you, Robin."

I stomped and pouted while we finished our shopping. Mom paid with food stamps, smiling and chatting up the person at the register. "She's getting tall," the woman said, motioning to me.

Mom rolled her eyes. "Can you believe it? In a few years she'll be taller than me!" They laughed. "Dani, say hi," Mom directed. She was always making sure that we used good manners around adults.

"Hi," I said, through gritted teeth.

"Ooooh, this one has a little attitude today!" the clerk said.

Mom looked down at me. "She'll get over it." Mom didn't seem to care that she had just given away more money than my piggy bank could ever hold, which just made me angrier.

"Here," she said, handing me a grocery bag. "Carry this."

As we walked home, I thought about the difference between Finders Keepers and stealing, and why the rules always seemed to mean that I ended up with nothing. Mom was right, of course—stealing was wrong. But this didn't feel like stealing; it wasn't like I reached in someone's pocketbook and took the money.

I didn't once consider how much character it took for a single mom on welfare with two kids to fork over a few hundred dollars to a man who surely kept the untraceable roll of bills to himself.

The larger lesson I learned was that the key to stealing was not telling anyone about it.

6.

The hardest thing to convey to my nieces and nephews about growing up is the concept of unadulterated freedom. My childhood had three modes—being at school, being asleep, and being the fuck out of my mom's way.

When I was growing up, a successful day was one where I saw my mother for *maybe* two hours total. Helicopter parents were born in the 1980s, a direct response to their personal experience of being roundly ignored by their own parents. Children were not to be seen or heard and were definitely not to complain about any injuries sustained during the fifteen hours a day we were roaming the streets. The 1980s were a decade of neglect, and I haven't felt freedom or terror like it since.

Summers on Jersey Avenue were wild. Not only did Mom avoid scheduling any day camps or babysitting, but she also had no earthly idea how we spent our time once she left for work. The only rule was that we were not allowed in our own house until she came home.

"Do not run in and out of this house all day with your friends," Mom said sternly. "I don't want you in here ruining this house." It was never clear to me what we could ruin or how we could ruin it since we had to ask her for permission to play with our own toys, but in Mom's mind, any child left alone in a house for more than three minutes was just looking for an excuse to rip couch cushions apart with their bare teeth.

I loved being inside. I could fill an entire day reading library books, creating new outfits for my Barbie out of candy wrappers, or practicing crochet chains with the giant ball of yarn my grandma gave me. Inside was full of wonder, mystery, and the life of the mind. Outside was a hellscape of mosquito bites, rusty nails, and scraped knees.

I once tried listing a slew of lurking emergencies for Mom in an effort to stay inside. Any one of them should have been enough for me to avoid nature, but she had a seemingly rational but ultimately insane response ready for every single question.

"What if I get thirsty?"

"There's a hose on the side of the Garretts' house."

"What if I get hungry?"

"You shouldn't be hungry before I come home from work."

"What if I have to poop?"

"Find a tree and a leaf."

"What if I break my arm?"

"Yell for help and someone will take you to the hospital."

"What if the person who comes to help me is a stranger? You said we should never go with or talk to strangers."

"If you ask me one more question you're punished for the rest of the night. *Go to bed*, Dani."

I hated being outside, but I loved the freedom that came with the extended parental neglect. With my only company being other children, I quickly became accustomed to a more feral way of life. We learned how to read a clock in school only for it to immediately become completely irrelevant; we rose with the sun, like farmers, and came in for the night when the streetlights turned on. The more ambitious among us laid out their play clothes the night before so they could jump into their outfits like firefighters about to tackle a blaze. The truly epic among us slept in their filthy clothes after a night of fighting with their parents about when it was time to come inside in the first place.

Even without arranging to meet, we all managed to wander out to the yards and streets of our neighborhoods around the same time, little Raisin Bran–fueled zombies. Sometimes you would hear a kid outside playing before anyone else, and that would be the clarion call to the rest of us to hustle. A cacophony of banging screen doors signaled our mass exodus. We were wild. We were free.

Mostly we were heathens who pissed outdoors for *months*.

Staying outside all day meant we had to find ways to be resourceful almost immediately. The biggest grift was trying to weasel your way into a bathroom. Stay-at-home moms everywhere lived by the same bible—No Child Left Inside.

Sometimes someone would summon the courage to just knock on a door and ask. The mom would answer and narrow her eyes suspiciously. "Number one or number two?" If it was number one, she'd just shake her head. "Outside," she'd say, pointing into the distance. "Can't have you kids running in here all day." If it was number two, she asked the cruelest question of all: "Can't you just hold it until you go home?" Even if your guts felt like a freshly wrung T-shirt, you instinctively knew that the answer was yes. It took a real psychopath to ask that question, and a real sociopath to say no.

Most of the time we just used any tree in any backyard. What did I use to wipe? Nothing at all, thank you very much. I tried to be careful, stretching my legs out as far as they would go, but I would invariably end up with a trickle of urine running down my leg, sometimes pooling in my Jellies. It was easy enough to spray down with a garden hose, even if there was no soap in sight; I just ran around smelling vaguely of piss until someone turned on a sprinkler for us to run through.

There was no privacy in outdoor pissing, thanks to tree houses, a lack of fences, and kids intent on catching you in the act. We had a song and everything:

> *I see your heinie*
> *So nice and shiny*
> *You better hide it*
> *Before I bite it*

Shitting was a nonissue. To my knowledge, there wasn't a child alive in the 1980s who ever took a shit all summer long.

My favorite part of summer was eating outside. It happened rarely; grilling wasn't the culturally trumped-up necessity that it is today, but on the super-hot days, no one wanted to turn on their ovens. If my mom was cooking, she'd sizzle some hot dogs in a frying pan, and then we'd carry them carefully outside and eat on the steps. Sometimes the fireflies would jump out at us, signaling the transition from dusk to night.

It was more of an affair when Mrs. Garrett was cooking. The Garretts had a yard and a picnic table that had once been a rustic red, now faded and patchy due to time and the elements. There were four kids in the Garrett family: Kerry, who was in high school and never ate with us; Timmy and Tommy, my brother's friends; and Erin, my best friend. The three boys were always waging a war against me and Erin, so getting us all to sit down together at a table was a mild miracle.

It was nice to be invited to eat with another family. The Garretts didn't have a dad either, but I never asked why. I liked the feeling of not having to explain that part of myself to someone else and thought Erin might feel the same way.

The thing I remember most about our outdoor picnics were Mrs. Garrett's nails. She never purchased hot dog or hamburger buns and insisted on using the loaf of white bread that was already on hand. She always put ketchup on the hamburgers whether you asked for it or not; her red, lacquered nails matched the ketchup pushing through the bread under the pressure of her hand.

The most memorable picnic started like any other: Mrs. Garrett flattened all of the food with her fingers, the boys were off on
the edge of the yard poking something with a stick, and Erin and
I ran around while we waited to eat. Mrs. Garrett brought out the
big plate of burgers, and we all crowded around the picnic table,
splinters shocking our thighs with every movement. For whatever
reason, I was seated next to Tommy that night, something I actively tried to avoid. He smelled like cheese and always had Oreo
stuff in his teeth. I found him repulsive. My mom was there, which
was a rarity, but her presence probably pushed our assigned seats
around a little.

I heard the swish of the lighter before I felt the fire. One second
I was eating a burger, and the next my mom was pushing me to the
ground and slapping my head. I started crying; I wasn't sure what
was happening or why I was suddenly getting beat up by my mom,
and I was terrified. She pulled me up to a standing position and
started looking at my head. Everyone at the table was silent.

"Why would you let him light your hair on fire like that?" Apparently Tommy had taken a lighter out of his pocket and lit the end
of one of my pigtails on fire. My mom saw it from across the table
and leapt into action.

My hair smelled like it always did whenever Grandma used the
hot comb, but the end of one pigtail was about an inch shorter than
the other. It felt crunchy on the end. "How could you let him do
that?" She was holding my head against her stomach, like she was
smothering flames that weren't there anymore. I was in a state of
disbelief; I didn't see the flames, and I accepted her version of what
happened but couldn't understand why I was the one in trouble.

Mrs. Garrett and the rest of the kids just stood frozen in place, unsure of what they would see when I could finally pull away. No one else even saw Tommy do it.

Mom was always getting it half right—she came to my rescue when I needed it but still found a way to blame me for needing to be rescued in the first place.

7.

There had been strict rules in place about how I was expected to act in public ever since I drifted away from my mom, Grandma, and Patsy at Sears when I was four years old. I thought it would be fun to play in the round rack of coats that I saw near the entrance, so when they weren't looking, I walked back down the aisle toward it, pushed two coats aside, and slid between them to the pole in the center. I walked around it in compact little circles, feeling all the soft fabric brush against my skin and humming a little song. It was my own private ring-around-the-rosy. I was in heaven until I heard Grandma shouting my name in the abrupt way that always meant I was about to be in big trouble—it was the same voice she used whenever she had to ask me to do anything more than once, like pick up my Legos from the living room, or move my Holly Hobbie doll out of the bathroom sink, where I was constantly dousing her fabric-covered head in water to try to wash it.

"Danielle Elizabeth Henderson! Get your ass over here!" she shouted. Grandma always used my full name when she was angry. None of the shoppers around her turned a head or lifted a finger to help; in the 1980s, department stores were full of people shouting the names of temporarily lost children, a cacophony of negligent parenting always ringing out like the last act of an opera.

She caught my eye as soon as I poked my head out from in between the coats, marched over, and dragged me out by the wrist. She was still holding my wrist when she leaned down and got right in my face. "If you run away like that one more time I'm going to let you stay lost. Do you want to live in this Sears?" Of course I wanted to live in Sears. It was full of toys and racks of clothes for me to play in, and my dipshit brother probably wouldn't be there. What a dumb question.

Instead of waiting for an answer, she walked me back over to my mom, who was still shopping, oblivious to my disappearance. "You better teach this child how to stay put," Grandma said, addressing the statement to me as she finally let go of my wrist. My mom, distracted by trying to locate the price tag on a pair of Jordache jeans, looked down at me. "Stand here," she said, pointing to a spot near her feet, "and if you move an inch I will *beat your ass*." That was the new rule, and she would use shorthand to remind me of it every time we were in a store from then on. "Not one inch," she'd say, the ass-beating part of the rule being implied.

Since I now had to stand next to my mom wherever we went, I got a closeup look at the way she carried herself in the world. The way she always said hello to strangers first and was prepared to have deeply involved conversations with everyone she met. Whenever she paid for something, I noticed the way she whispered the bill and coin denominations out loud and counted them twice, just to make sure they were accurate. She always knew exactly where everything was in any store and was quick to stop and help people who looked lost. Everywhere we went, people treated her like they were meeting a moon goddess who had floated down to earth just to make their day.

It was wild to see the effect my mom had on people. She was gorgeous, with her blinding smile and big brown eyes. She had a loud laugh that always petered out to a gentle sigh; her laugh had a way of making you feel like you were the funniest person in the galaxy. It made me proud to see how much people liked her. And since I came directly out of her uterus, I felt like I was beautiful and funny by proximity, even if nothing could be further from the truth. If she let her light shine on someone else for a minute too long, my stomach would tingle, my head started to hurt. My body reacted painfully when it felt like Mom might forget me.

I tried to remind her that I was there, too. I would try to tug on her jeans, but she always wore them tight; instead of grabbing fabric, I'd end up accidentally pinching her thigh. "Ow, Dani!" She'd look down at me, still smiling but pulling the muscles of her forehead together so tight I could tell by her eyes that she was angry. She'd laugh it off with her stranger, talking about me rather than talking to me. "This one, she's *so* impatient. I can't get a minute to myself! Jeez O'Flip!"

Both Mom and Grandma used this weird version of Jesus H. Christ, shortening it and, for some reason, making it kind of Irish. I can't imagine my grandma ever avoiding a chance to curse, but like all complicated women, she seems to have felt a duty to keep it classy in public. When my mom said, "Jeez O'Flip!" it sounded like a cute country phrase, like someone hopped out of an episode of *The Andy Griffith Show* and straight into upstate New York. When my grandma said it, it looked like that part of *Men in Black* where the alien is trying on his Vincent D'Onofrio suit for the first time and trying to act normal. She muttered it, like she was trying to keep a load of acrid bile from dribbling out of the corner of her mouth.

No matter what made-up language Mom used, the sentiment wasn't lost on me—my constant need for her attention was a hindrance. My existence kept Mom from being the breezy, unencumbered twenty-eight-year-old she really wanted to be.

I craved my mom, even when she was standing right next to me. With her hand in mine and my head resting on her hip, I wondered what I could do to make her feel as light as she seemed to be with everyone else. I wanted her to gently touch my arm and laugh at my knock-knock jokes the way she did when strangers said anything at all. What would it feel like to have my mom all to myself?

For the rest of my life, I would never know the answer.

Mom treated everyone the same; she was a universal flirt. Women liked her; they could relate to her as a parent or talk about old times at Monroe-Woodbury High School. Everyone in Greenwood Lake pretty much stayed put, so most of the women we ran into had known Mom since she moved there as a kid.

Men were different when they talked to Mom. They lingered too long, stared too intently. Every once in a while one of them would lean down and try to ask me a question to show that hey, he was cool with kids. "And what grade are you in?"

Situations like this helped me on my way to perfecting a withering glare. I'd stare at them and through gritted teeth say, "I'm not allowed to talk to strangers." How was this not universal knowledge, chump? If she was interested in the guy, Mom would nudge my shoulder. "That's not very nice, Dani," she'd say, then flash her big teeth at him while I stood next to her, hoping I could burn through him with my eyes the same way the floating people in the glitter jumpsuits did in the second Superman movie.

I cut my feminist teeth on men who thought they could impress Mom by acknowledging my existence. Men were boring to me at best and threatening at worst. In trying to use me to woo Mom, they often lost the game before they even uttered a word. I didn't want them to see me; I wanted her, without anyone else around to butt in.

It was like that for a while. The three of us, Mom, Cory, and me, a cohesive unit. She didn't have much time for dating, and that was fine with me. So you can imagine my surprise when I woke up one morning to a man in the house.

It was morning, and our bedroom door was closed. It was never closed, not since Grandma showed us *The Blob* and I started having panic attacks at bedtime. I needed the door to stay open so that I could make my escape the moment I saw the first drop of pink sludge hanging in the doorway. We had a Tot Finder sticker in our window for firemen, but we didn't have a Blob Finder sticker, because no one survived the fucking Blob. Mom didn't have the time or patience for my Blob-related fears.

"It's not coming for you!" she screamed, her voice hitting the high pitch it always did when she was about to lose her patience.

"Mom, it's coming for *all of us*—that's what it does!" There was no reasoning with her.

I opened our bedroom door with the full expectation that everything had been consumed during the night.

Mom was intact. But she wasn't alone. A man was next to her on the couch, his naked torso visible above the sheet that covered them both. I ran back into the bedroom and woke up Cory.

"Someone's here!" I whispered. We both tiptoed out to the living room. I was pointing at the sleeping figure and whispering a little too loudly when suddenly Mom popped up. "Go back to sleep!" she hissed, loud enough to make the guy next to her rustle. As a family, we had a lot to learn about whispering. "And close the door!"

Cory and I went back to our room, where we spent what seemed like ages trying to figure out what was going on. We'd never met our dad, and my granddad worked all the time, so we weren't used to seeing two adults sleeping next to each other. Our conspiracies ranged from a burglar ("But she would call the cops") to a new dad ("Then why can't we talk to him?"). I was too hungry to keep waiting, so I peeked out the bedroom door.

The living room was back to normal. Mom was folding her blanket and sheet, and the curtains were open. Sun streamed through the living room; dust motes glinted in the rays. Mom was very casual. "Do you want cereal?"

One, of course we wanted cereal—I would eat Cap'n Crunch for every single meal if I was allowed, and the fact that Mom constantly told me to stop asking her if I could have a bowl was a clear indication that I wanted cereal all day, every day. Two, was anyone going to address the man we just saw in here?

"Mom, who was that?"

"Who was who?"

Parents, don't try this shit. It's insulting to your child's intelligence and makes you look like a straight-up criminal.

"That *man*," Cory chimed in.

"Oh, that was my friend Tony. He spent the night." Mom was totally nonchalant. Meanwhile, I felt like someone had tugged a string in my skull and was pulling my brain out through my throat.

"BUT WHO IS HE." I demanded answers. You can't just bring a stranger in here, have him sleep on the foundation of my pillow fort, and not explain who he is or if he's coming back.

Mom stopped folding the sheet and threw it on the couch. "Goddammit, I told you—his name is Tony. He's my friend. That's all you need to know, so stop asking me questions about it, Jeez O'Flip! I'm allowed to have friends."

I was livid for two reasons: First of all, I thought I knew all of Mom's friends. Uncle Joe and Aunt Jeannie, who she'd been friends with since their drum corps days in high school; Paula, who lived across the driveway in one of the cottages and had recently started working part-time at Pendine with Mom and Grandma as a way to bring in some extra money and stave off boredom; my aunt and uncle. Those were her friends, and Tony never factored in.

I was also very upset because Cory and I weren't allowed to have sleepovers, so why the fuck was she breaking her own rule like it was no big deal?

"Well," I said, assuming the floodgates were open, "if you can have a sleepover, can I have a sleepover? With Erin?" Not only did she fail to see my logic, Mom thought I was being a smartass. "No, Erin can't sleep over, and go stand in the corner for talking back to me."

So far this Tony guy was making my life a real pain in the ass.

Cory and I eventually met Tony during daylight hours. He was goofy and funny. Tony had the same skin tone as mine, but his curly hair wasn't as thick or as coarse. His mustache didn't cover his acne-scarred cheeks. He looked friendly, like he wouldn't mind my questions; I didn't know what acne was at that point, so I asked him if he got his scars from picking scabs. "My grandma always yells at me for picking my knee scabs because of scars. But I like scars!" Without realizing it, I was trying to endear myself to him, to find some similarities. "Well, yeah," he said, "I guess I got them from picking scabs. Listen to your grandma," he said with a small laugh.

Listen to the meanest, craziest person I'd ever met who was intent on scaring the shit out of me as much as possible? He clearly hadn't met my grandma yet.

It can't have been easy for my mom to date. There were slim pickings in Greenwood Lake, and she had the added bonus of having two kids. Most of her friends were people she'd known since high school—not the greatest dating pool, or the best people to set you up with someone outside of your social circle. She must have felt lonely, or at least thought about how she could possibly be alone for the rest of her life. But I wasn't sorry when Tony stopped coming around one day.

Mom's flirting was starting to impact my life majorly by the time I was in third grade. My gym teacher, Mr. Folino, was, by her determination, a hunk. Personally I didn't see the appeal. His brown hair was parted in the middle and feathered around his ears; he never did the buttons on his Le Tigre logo shirts, so there was always a patch of hair sprouting out toward his collar. The gold Italian horn necklace he always wore was plopped right in the middle of that distracting thatch. It looked like a tiny scribble, a wiggly little omen.

They met when she came to pick me up from school one day, and every time she knew I had gym, she'd ask about him. "How is Mr. Folino? What a hunk." If there was anything I hated more than gym, it was the word "hunk." It sounded like an illness. "James can't come to school today; he's a hunk." I knew it had been a while since my mom was in grade school, but there's no way I would

ever know how Mr. Folino was doing. Did she think I was saun-
tering into class, grabbing the edge of the giant parachute we flapped
around and counted as physical education, and having an in-depth
conversation with him about his weekend or if he preferred Folgers over Chock full o' Nuts? I had tried talking to a teacher like a
regular human being once, right after Mrs. Puca said she would
read me the riot act for poking Neil Scarfuro in the hand with my
pencil when he tried to steal one of my Garbage Pail Kids cards.
"What's the riot act?" I asked innocently. "What book is it in? Can
I read it myself?" I genuinely thought it was a scrolled text she
kept in her desk drawer. She got so angry that she made me stay
after school and wash the chalkboards with a giant sponge, and I
never asked her another question that wasn't related to something
in our workbooks. As far as I was concerned, when kids emptied
the building, all of the teachers folded their arms across their chests
as they were locked in Dracula-like storage cabinets for the night.
They didn't exist outside of school, and they certainly weren't people that my mom should be horny about.

For his part, Mr. Folino rather inappropriately asked about my
mom once. We had just spent an entire gym class rolling around
on wooden boards with wheels—you sat on the board, then pushed
yourself around with your hands and feet. The only goal of this
game was, seemingly, to move around for forty minutes, crushing
our fingers under the wheels as we whizzed past one another like
little maniacs. Once a year we'd be forced outside to do something
called the Presidential Fitness Test; since we spent most of the year
doing parachutes, wheelie boards, and fuck all that would count as
exercise, my classmates and I wheezed our way around the building

and tried to pull our malnourished, underdeveloped bodies above pull-up bars in order to prove to the president that our skeletons weren't going to break from a gust of strong wind. It was mayhem, a bunch of little Benjamin Buttons exhausting ourselves over the kind of exercise we wouldn't do again for another solid calendar year.

I was stacking my wheelie board and resetting my cracked knuckles when Mr. Folino asked about my mom. "How's, uh, how's your ma doing?" It's a wonder to me that anyone in the 1980s found a way to procreate with opening lines like this, spoken to your intended's child.

"She's at work," I said sternly.

"Tell her I said hi," Mr. Folino said, jogging backward toward the stage. It's possible I thwarted one of the great loves of our time, but if either of these chumps thought I was going to pass along messages, they were dead fucking wrong.

My school did a concert every year, which was a simple way of saying, hey, come to school at night and watch your kids bounce around on the stage for an hour. My class was doing a dance routine set to Whitney Houston's "How Will I Know," which was as devastatingly uncoordinated as you may imagine. Mom got me a "cute" outfit for the event—white silk shorts with vertical red lines and a matching red shirt—and I did my best to learn the choreography. The bane of my existence is that I have perfect rhythm but no actual moves; I can keep a beat, but I failed to learn how to dance as a way of self-expression. Some people enjoy moving their bodies with precision; I just don't have that kind of joy in my heart.

Mr. Folino took one look at my spastic motions and decided I should be front and center. "Your ma will love it," he said, snapping his gum. I told him that I didn't want to be in front, but it was nonnegotiable.

On the night of the concert, it wouldn't have mattered if I stood on the stage screaming verse in Latin straight to the sky—Mom only had eyes for Mr. Folino. I tripped and stumbled my way through the routine, bumping into my friends Jeannette and Erin every time I tried to turn around. When it was over, I slunk off the stage and found Mom in the crowd.

"You did great," she said as she hugged me. But I could tell by the angle of her chin on the top of my head that she was looking at him.

8.

The summer I turned seven, we had moved across the hall to the bigger two-bedroom apartment. Mom gave me and Cory our own rooms, and she still slept on the couch. She must have felt like it was time to spruce things up now that we had a new place, so it was decided that Cory and I would go to California for the summer to stay with my aunt Rene. It was pitched to us as an adventure, but I was instantly nervous about the flight for two distinctly uncontrollable reasons: my rapidly growing fear of heights and terrorism.

There were constant reports of terrorists and plane hijackings on the nightly news; they didn't go into detail, but Cory did his best to fill in the blanks. "They take barbed wire and run it up and down your bare legs," he said matter-of-factly. "You know how they always ask for women and children? It's so they can kill you first." I tried to argue with his rationale by reminding him that he, too, was a child. "But I'm a boy," he said. "Even if they tried to get me they'd still torture you first, because you're a women *and* a children." Cory had me so consumed by thoughts of airplane torture that I didn't even focus on how I was going to spend two months in a different state without my mom.

Eventually I started to get sad that Mom would be alone all summer, so she did her best to contain her soon-to-be-alone glee by reminding us that she was going to be busy at work. "I'm going to do a lot of overtime and really get this place fixed up," she'd sing, floating around like Snow White while birds landed on her fingers. She seemed so happy I asked if she would actually miss us. "Yeah, of course I'll miss you," she said, gripping a measuring tape in her mouth as she pushed me out of the way.

We went out to California in style. Since no one drove or had a car, Grandma rented a stretch limo to take us to Newark Airport. Any dreams I had of re-creating a lavish heavy metal video were dashed the minute our bags were loaded in the trunk. "Listen to me—you are not allowed to touch anything in here, do you hear me?" Grandma got right in my face while the driver waited patiently, holding the door open. "If you touch anything we'll turn this car right back around and you'll spend the summer on my couch." I turned myself into a statue. If you had painted me gold or silver I could have stood in Central Park with a bucket, collecting loose change.

Mom and Grandma walked us right up to the gate and put us on the plane. I remember eyeballing everyone as they boarded to see if I could pick out which one was going to storm the cockpit and slice my legs open, but I don't actually remember the plane ride out there. It's possible I passed out from the stress.

My aunt was always a fascinatingly cool woman. After high school, she moved to Middletown with a couple of friends and attended Orange County Community College, about forty minutes away from Greenwood Lake. A year later, she drove cross-country to California with three friends. Of the original group, she was the only one still there, working retail, paying rent, and having fun. She was the manager of a record store, and when we talked to her on the phone she always seemed to be on her way to a concert or out with friends.

Aunt Rene lived in Fairfield, north of San Francisco, in one of three apartment buildings that formed a U-shape around a rectangular pool. Everything was beige and sun-bleached, including the carpet in her top-floor apartment. The place was bigger than ours—relentless sunshine through the sliding glass door of her small balcony kissed every surface in her large living room, and her galley-style kitchen had an area big enough for a table at the end, near the window facing the pool. Two bedrooms jutted off a small hallway just beyond the living room, and the bathroom was tucked in at the end, across from the bigger bedroom. In less than a week, I'd find out that the storage closet in between the bedroom and bathroom was big enough for two kids to play in all day.

She loved music; the radio or record player was always going. Photos of friends were framed on the wall in the hallway. Severe-looking Robert Nagel posters hung on the living room walls, and she had rows of records stacked up next to the entertainment system, stretching halfway into the living room. She even let us look at them, which is how I saw my first dick.

I picked up the one with the purple cover, drawn in by the cartoons splattered across the front. Cartoons instantly meant "this is something for kids," so I carefully plucked it out of its row and started to see what I could read. "Prince. Who is that?" Aunt Rene pulled the record out of its sleeve and popped it on the turntable, dropping the needle on the song "1999."

Over the course of the summer I'd memorize the opening of that song, often entering the room by holding out my arms and saying, "Dearly beloved . . ." I loved the music but was still transfixed by the album cover. Even though the three nines were all done in a crazy style, I recognized them as numbers. The one, though . . . I had no idea what that was. "Hey, Aunt Rene, what is this?" I said, pointing to the stick with the round-helmet shape on top. "It doesn't look like a number."

Cory poked his head over my shoulder and started laughing. "That's a wiener!" he said, laughing and pointing. "That. Is. A. Wienerrrrr." Like all little boys, Cory was jazzed by any chance to talk about dicks in polite company. And he wasn't wrong; staring at me from the flat, purple background, the number one in the *1999* title was a cartoon penis so vibrant that it looked like it was on an acid trip. I'd seen Cory's wang a couple of years before, when

Mom still plopped us in the bathtub together; it didn't look anything like the dick on Prince's album.

Aunt Rene wasn't the least bit fazed by the sight of her niece holding a semi-filthy record and asking about dicks. She casually walked over to us from the kitchen, looked at the record, and said, "Yeah, that's a wiener, Dani," and walked back into the kitchen, laughing.

Mom, Grandma, and Rene all had the same joy-filled laugh—I just heard it more often at my aunt's house. I didn't know what stress was at the time, but looking back, I think she didn't have much of it. Her apartment was always filled with laughter, and she thought Cory and I were funny. She was patient with my questions and never told me to leave her alone. When her friends came by the apartment, they always greeted her with a strong hug before they all recounted stories about this one night out, or remember that day at the store? Her life was full of more than just family.

Things were going to be different in California.

Uncle Bobby had moved in with Aunt Rene a few months before we arrived. He wanted to follow in his sister's footsteps, but he didn't have a job yet, so he was in charge of watching us all summer since he was home all day. It made sense on paper, but nothing could have made less sense in actuality. Bobby was in his mid-twenties at the time, hoping to come to California to wild out and find himself; instead, he had to spend all day making sure neither Cory nor I drowned in the pool.

He mostly treated us with malicious neglect. Unlike Mom, he didn't even pretend to care if we lived or died. "Who cares," he'd say when I ran to him, whining about something horrible Cory did or said. Everything we did was confusing to him. When we asked him to make us eggs for breakfast, he sincerely asked, "Don't you know how to make it yourself?" as if we were ever allowed near a stove unsupervised. When we asked if we could go out to play in an unfamiliar city with unfamiliar streets, he'd say, "Yes, go, I don't care, do what you want." I was used to being alone at home—I knew the streets, and I knew the people. I had a turf, with built-in boundaries. But I also knew when I was allowed to come home or how to get to Mom if there was a problem. This was different; I didn't know what to do if I got in trouble or needed someone to help. What if I got lost? The apartment complex was full of strangers—I didn't know anyone. I didn't even know what kind of trouble California offered.

One of the women who worked with my aunt also lived in the same apartment building, and she had a daughter around my age. Bianca seemed tiny; in retrospect, she was probably considered average, but by age seven I already had legs as long as a giraffe. She wore her hair pulled back in the same tight braids and dangling barrettes as I did, and she could make an actual muscle when she flexed her wiry arms. Her two front teeth were missing, giving an adorably puckish appearance to her already pretty face.

We were a unit, the two of us. Sometimes we tried to torment Cory, but mostly we played by ourselves. Bianca brought her Barbies up from her place; her mom worked with my aunt at the record store but also had an additional job, so she slept a lot during the day. We weren't allowed to play at Bianca's, so we dragged her toys and dolls up to Aunt Rene's, much to the dismay of my uncle.

"There's not enough of your shit here, now you have to bring in hers?" he'd say in a huff, pointing at the Barbies as he walked to the kitchen.

I had a real deference to adults and authority thanks to my grandma, but Bianca wasn't raised by her grandparents.

"I'm only going to be here while we play. *GOD*." Bianca rolled her eyes and turned away from him, neither expecting nor waiting for a response.

My uncle was acting like a petulant teenager, but he never expected a petulant preteen to give him a dose of his own attitude. Uncle Bobby stalked off to his room with his coffee and slammed the door. Bianca made a face behind his back as he passed, sticking her tongue out.

I worshipped her.

Bianca was my first Black friend. I didn't have to explain my cornrows to her or talk about how my hair would shrink up if we ever decided to swim in the pool. I didn't have the language to describe how exciting it was, so instead I described how all the people in my town were white. Other than my brush with the Weiringers, no one in my orbit really talked about race. I knew my family was Black, and that other Black people existed, but that was about it. As a kid who lived in a relatively diverse midsize city, Bianca couldn't understand how it was possible to live in a purely white world.

"All of them?" she asked, waving a Barbie doll back and forth on the floor to mimic footsteps.

"All of them. Except for me and my brother and my mom and my grandma and granddad," I said, digging through the pile of tiny clothes.

Bianca wrinkled her nose. "That sounds bad."

I'd never really thought about it much, but through her eyes, I could see that Greenwood Lake left a lot to be desired. I wanted her to think I was cool, so I agreed. "Yeah, it's bad."

As soon as the words left my mouth I felt the first twinges of betrayal. I tried to backtrack—there was a lake, and my teacher Mrs. Dietzel let us make a teepee out of a big roll of brown paper where we could read during quiet time.

"But you're the only Black people?" Bianca asked.

I nodded.

She made the Barbie hop on the carpet. "Well, you look white, so . . ." She didn't finish the sentence, but I didn't need her to.

Aunt Rene flew to New York with us at the end of the summer. The plane ride back was much more relaxing; Aunt Rene shut down Cory's tales of terrorism, so we just played with coloring books and drank as much soda as they would bring us.

When Cory and I got back to Jersey Avenue, our apartment was totally transformed. Light blue wall-to-wall carpet flowed through the living room under a brand-new couch and TV. My bed had a new comforter, and we both had new curtains. My mom beamed with pride showing us all the new stuff. "I worked overtime all summer," she said, pointing to the TV. Everything she got was practical; there were no overflowing toy boxes or brand-new video games, but somehow this was better. We had an apartment that was full of stuff that my mom picked out, stuff that wasn't handed down. For the first time, everything was ours.

Aunt Rene couldn't believe that Cory and I had never been to the Museum of Natural History, so we took a bus to the city with Grandma and Mom one day in late August to fix that.

I talked everyone's ear off the entire two-hour bus ride down to the city, so that by the time we got to the Port Authority, everyone was already exhausted and snappy. Grandma almost broke my hand holding me close as we walked the eight blocks down to Thirty-Fourth Street, dodging men pushing their entire lives in carts, people wearing underwear as pants, and women in skirt suits and white Easy Spirit sneakers charging through the crowds. We'd only been to the city once before this, to visit Sweetie Pie. It had been a hurried trip, and we weren't there to explore. This visit was vivid from the moment we stepped off the bus.

Grandma wore the wrong shoes; her feet hurt already, so we went off as a group toward Macy's so that she could buy some sneakers. I gawked and stared at everything. By the time we traversed the eight blocks to get there, I'd already seen an entire universe of people that were nowhere to be found in Greenwood Lake.

Grandma was used to Cory and me running around department

stores in the mall; she did her usual don't-act-like-an-idiot shopping speech with added urban flavor. "This is New York City," she said, leaning in front of me and Cory. "If you run away from me here, someone *will* snatch you. When they steal kids in the city, they sell them to new families or cut them up into little pieces. We'll never be able to find you. So if you want to run around today, well, it's been nice knowing you." She stood up and craned her neck around to find Mom and Aunt Rene while I considered if the new family I'd be sold into would let me have an Atari.

We walked through the crowded store to the escalator, one of the most talked-up aspects of this trip. "Oh, I love that old escalator," Aunt Rene said, beaming, on the bus. "It's really cool." As an adult, I can appreciate the beauty of the old, wooden escalator that Macy's maintains, but as a child, it was a clanking nightmare machine. My entire family hopped on as if it were a ride at Six Flags, but I took one look at the teeth-like way the slats grinded together and hesitated. "Come *on*, Dani," Grandma called from a few feet up. As my family started to move away from me, I had two choices: jump on the clanking, growling death machine, or possibly get kidnapped and cut up by a stranger. I hesitated before tentatively stepping on.

When I got to the top, they were all waiting for me like a firing squad. Mom had effectively taken the day off from parenting, so Grandma was the one to grab my upper arm and pull me so close I could smell the last cigarette she smoked as she spoke through gritted teeth. "What did I just say? You better stay close to us, you hear me?"

I hung close as we made our way to the shoe department. Grandma was picking up sneakers and sucking her teeth at the un-

believable price of every pair. "Fifty dollars? We can get these at
Sears for half the price." Grandma never wanted us to leave the
house looking like "ragamuffins," but the price system on raga-
muffosity had a strict limit. "You kids grow so damn fast," she said,
putting the sneaker back on its plastic pedestal. "What's the point
of spending so much? You're just going to outgrow them in two
months." As she whisked us through the store looking for the cheap-
est, cleanest pair of sneakers Macy's had to offer, I noticed my mom
and aunt were talking to someone.

He was very tall, with a short afro and clean-shaven face. I only
caught a glimpse of him, but he had a wide smile. Aunt Rene walked
away, looking annoyed, as my mom stood there, grinning. Aunt
Rene came back over to us, and Grandma launched into her interrogation.

"Who is that?"

Aunt Rene rolled her eyes. "No one. Some man. He asked
me out."

"What did you say?"

"I said no, Ma! Now he's talking to Robin." Aunt Rene was
disgusted. "See that little old lady next to him? That's his mother—
she's buying him shoes."

Grandma laughed. "Robin doesn't have the sense the good lord
gave her."

When Mom finally came back over to us, she was holding his
phone number on a tiny piece of paper. "He's nice," she insisted
when met with Grandma's and Aunt Rene's scowls.

"Robin, a nice man doesn't pick you up in Macy's while you're
shopping with your children," Grandma said.

"A nice man doesn't need his elderly mother to buy him shoes, either," Aunt Rene said under her breath.

But Mom was happy. She'd met a man. Luke. And it didn't matter that he'd just hit on her little sister moments before asking for her phone number. Luke was going to call her, and she was elated.

He called.

He came to visit.

He never left.

9.

Luke just showed up one weekend, all smiles and hugs. Probably took the New Jersey Transit bus right to the corner and got off in front of the library where I once went to preschool. He was huge, the tallest person I'd ever met, with skin the same color as mine, and he was standing in the doorway to our apartment. It had been about two weeks since Macy's, and Mom didn't tell us he was coming. He didn't bring Cory and me anything to show goodwill or even acknowledge that we existed; he just appeared, with an army duffel bag full of clothes.

As soon as he arrived, he started in on us. "These kids have their own bedrooms? And you sleep on the couch?" He sucked his teeth as if to say, *You sucker*, like we'd won the rooms from my mom in a poker bet. "Man, these kids are spoiled." That was his go-to insult for us regarding the few things we owned that we could call ours. "They're not spoiled," Mom said lightly.

"Mm-hmm," Luke said, eyeing the toy box in Cory's room.

It was unsettling, having a man's presence in our lives. Different from Granddad, who was soft and kind. Luke left the whiff of a threat everywhere.

Luke slept next to Mom on the pullout couch in the living room and usually stayed in bed after she went to work. Grandma didn't come over in the mornings anymore; instead, we fumbled around in the dark for our clothes and snuck out as softly as possible, not even wanting the doorknob to make a noise when we turned it.

We had to be quiet, or else Luke yelled at us a lot. Growing up in apartments meant we were always cognizant of our noise levels; I've never stomped up a set of stairs a day in my life, and it's still difficult for me to raise my voice above regular speaking tones when I'm inside. The way Luke reacted to us made it seem like we were holding marching band auditions in our bedrooms instead of playing a game of Trouble.

One day after school, Cory and I were on the floor in his room playing with a deck of cards. Mom was at work, so we had a couple of hours before she came home and made us do our homework. War was a favorite game, just turning over cards to see who had the highest number; if you both put down the same card, you laid three cards facedown and turned over the fourth to see who won that round. But it didn't count if you failed to say "I. De. Clare.

WAR!" with every card you placed. Winning a War round was intense, because it meant you got to scoop up all the cards.

We were excited, because we'd had an epic DOUBLE WAR— when we flipped over our fourth cards, they also matched. We shouted at the sky, unable to believe the mathematical odds or cosmic interference that would result in one of us winning a shitload of cards. Then we heard Luke's footsteps.

Cory's bedroom door swung open so hard it hit the wall. Luke's brown eyes were blazing, his forehead an angry mess of lines. "Shut the *fuck*. *Up*." We were stunned, immobile, as he marched over to our pile of cards and picked them all up. "I'm sick of hearing you two." He carried the cards out of the room. I started to cry. Quietly.

"Shut up, you baby," Cory whispered through his sneer. "If he hears you crying, he's just going to come back and yell at us again."

Grandma yelled at us when she was irritated; she made threats as a way to get us to calm down or get out of her way, but I still never felt like there was actual violence on the horizon. Luke's threats were more chilling; we weren't part of him, and he didn't have to love us. He was a stranger. And if there was one thing I knew for sure, it was that strangers had a bad habit of hurting kids.

We fell into a new routine. We stayed outside for as long as we could after school, while Mom was at work, until the other kids started getting called in to do homework or eat dinner. Sometimes I did homework with Erin and waited until her mom started putting dinner on the table to cut through the yard and go back to the apartment. Mom was usually home by then.

I never knew what I was going to get when I opened the door. Sometimes Luke was still sleeping, as if he hadn't moved from the couch all day. Other times he'd be watching TV. The best times were the ones when he wasn't there at all; I fantasized about the earth swallowing him up, the same way the bed ate that boy in *A Nightmare on Elm Street*.

One day I came home and the TV was on. Luke was sitting on the couch, so I tried to scoot by him into my bedroom.

"Dani, watch this."

I didn't know how to say no to him and didn't want to make him angry, so I dropped down on the couch as far away from him as possible, pushing my body into the arm so hard the fabric left a pattern on my shoulder.

The movie on the television didn't look like anything I'd ever seen. It was quieter than a horror movie and just looked like a bunch of people sitting around a kitchen table. I looked over at Luke; he was grinning, his eyes fixed to the screen. "The good part is coming up."

Someone was holding a screeching monkey, and they lowered it into a hole in the middle of the table. It was screaming, its teeth bared and its eyes wildly looking around the room. Then someone took a mallet and hit it on the head. I closed my eyes and pushed my head into my shoulder, but I could hear the monkey being hit on the head again.

"You're missing it! They're eating the brains." Luke was giddy.

Of all the horror movies I'd watched, this felt viscerally different. My stomach lurched like it did when I needed to puke.

"They're eating the brains." He laughed with his whole body; I could feel him bouncing around on the end of the couch. Watching *Faces of Death* was a sport for him; who knew how many times he'd seen it. His joy was perverse; as much as I feared his anger, his happiness in the face of destruction made me want to crawl out of my skin.

When it sounded like it was over, I turned to him without looking at the TV. "Can I go to my room now? I have homework."

"You're no fun," Luke said, frowning.

I didn't have a sense of humor when he started coming into my room at night, either, while everyone else was asleep.

We had lived in the apartment for only a few months, but its shiny promise was already tarnished by Luke's dangerous, demanding body. The couch might have looked the same way it did when Mom first brought it home, the dull turquoise slashes still vibrant against the heathered gray fabric, but Luke had ruined it by draping himself over it like he owned it, his heavy body a constant presence. I longed for our apartment across the hall, where everything had been ours to cover in string, where the only fear of the night was a fictional horror movie character emblazoned a little too brightly in my brain. Luke was becoming a permanent stain on our lives.

It was normal to be spanked. If you survived the eighties without getting hit, your parents were probably the kind of hippies who referred to your bursts of disobedience as an exploration of your wild spirit and believed that love energy was a powerful way to stop nukes from launching. Mom often lost her patience with us; we were loud and didn't have enough space to respect each other's boundaries. Our spankings weren't prolonged affairs; Mom usually stomped over to wherever we were misbehaving, grabbed an arm to spin us around, and delivered a quick pop of a smack to the fleshy part of an ass. She didn't pull down our pants or make us get branches from the yard the way some parents did—it was more of a brief, merciful warning of her power, strength, and control. A reminder that we had our place, and she had hers.

Cory was probably doing something annoying the day that our spankings changed. He was playing in his room, smashing plastic toys against each other and imitating explosions with his mouth. I could hear him from the couch, where I was trying to read a book while Mom did something in the kitchen. Luke, asleep in my bed, stormed into the living room. "Robin," he yelled, "tell that kid to shut up!" The wall between our bedrooms was distractingly thin; I could hear Cory's legs shift under crisp sheets when we were trying to fall asleep at night.

Mom popped her head out of the kitchen. "Luke, it's the middle of the day. He's playing." You could hear the exhaustion in her voice, but this was about as much as she ever challenged him—a wan, monotone sentence with expressionless eyes. Luke always met her exhaustion with bombastic proclamations, ratcheting up his already loud voice to an apartment-shaking boom. "I'm trying to sleep—if you don't shut that kid up, I will."

I kept my face in my book, so afraid to even blink that the words blurred together from the strength of my stare. If I didn't move, they wouldn't know I was listening.

Mom and Luke went back to their corners, boxers taking a break in a round with no clear winner. My tension was knowing that no conversations ever ended this smoothly. Nothing was over until Luke got what he wanted.

A few minutes later, he stormed back out of my bedroom, this time holding a belt. He crossed the living room in two steps and stood in the doorway, brandishing the limp belt in front of him. "I told you—if you don't, I will." I heard some pans clatter as Mom stopped what she was doing. She tried to push past Luke, but he stood in the doorway and refused to move.

Mom tried to slide past him, ducking her head under his arm-pit. "I'm not hitting him for playing, Luke," she said. He grabbed her arm and held it straight out behind her. I peeked over my book, triggered by the small, sharp sound she made as she twisted her body around to face him. They stood close. He was still holding her wrist when he lifted the belt in his other hand and said, "What, you want me to beat you to show you how it's done?" His smile was supposed to make her think he was joking, but his peaked eye-brows told another story. He was menacing, a word I wouldn't learn for another few years.

Whatever Mom saw in his face made her grab the belt out of his hand. She walked into Cory's room and closed the door. "Turn around," she said brusquely, "and pull down your pants." Cory tried to ask why, and she must have done her patented arm-spinning move to get his backside facing her.

Mom emphasized certain words with every smack of the belt. "You are TOO LOUD in here. I TOLD you to BE quiet when you're PLAYING and LUKE is SLEEPING." Cory screamed with every lick of the leather against his skin. My throat stung, like a hot rock was painfully lodged in there. I felt tears dripping down to my neck. With Luke, I learned how to cry without making a sound.

Cory was still scream-crying when Mom left his room. She shoved the belt at Luke on her way back to the kitchen. My invisibility shield crumbled when I sniffed back some tear-based snot. Mom snapped her head toward me. Her face was a mix of anger and sadness; her eyebrows were pinched together in the middle, but her mouth was shaking.

"What are you crying about?" she hissed. "You're not even the one who got the spanking."

The person talking was foreign to me. She looked like Mom, but I'd never heard her so twisted and cruel. She sniffed and wiped her eye as she walked past me. I listened to Cory cry through his bedroom door as Mom walked into the bathroom, and I couldn't figure out which one scared me more.

Luke and Mom started going to the city a lot. He'd fold his huge body behind the wheel of our car and Mom would climb into the passenger seat. I hated seeing him in the Honda, hated that Mom let him drive. They usually came back before bedtime, and we were pretty okay on our own in the meantime; I liked to read my

library books and eat Funyuns that I got from Hanley's, and Cory
would run around with the Garretts until he got hungry. Sometimes Mom would leave us salami-and-cheese sandwiches on
white bread for dinner. Sometimes she forgot, and we didn't eat
dinner.

One night, Mom put us to bed. She read with each of us and
kissed our foreheads goodnight, her necklace clinking against my
cheek when she leaned in. I fell asleep pretty quickly and didn't
hear her leave the apartment with Luke. A loud noise woke me up,
and I went out to the living room. No one was there.

I opened the door to Cory's room and woke him up. "Mom
isn't here," I whispered.

"So what?" Cory was never good at waking up, but this seemed
like cause for alarm, and I needed his help.

"What should I do?"

"Go back to sleep!"

Suddenly very aware that I was in the dark, basically alone, I
started to panic. With no adult to protect us, anything could get
me in here—the Blob, the Creature from the Black Lagoon, Michael Myers. All of the horror movie villains from Grandma's TV
sprang to the front of my mind, along with every teenager they
murdered along the way. I started crying. I walked to the kitchen,
turned on the light, and dialed Grandma's number.

"Dani? Why are you calling me so late?"

I had no idea what time it was; it was just dark o'clock. "Do you
know when my mom is coming home?"

"She's not there with you?" Grandma's voice was a mix of panic
and anger. "Where is she?"

"I don't know," I wailed, the tears coming out uncontrollably now.

"Where's Cory?"

"He's aslee-ee-eeeep." I was crying so hard I started to hiccup in between sobs.

"Dani, hang up the phone. I'm coming. Don't answer the door for anyone but me."

I hung up and went to my room to calm down and wait for her.

Grandma knocked on the door a little bit later. As soon as I opened it, she grabbed me in a hug. The sheer force of her made me start crying again. She pushed me away at arm's length so that she could grab my shoulders and look me in the eye. "Go get some clothes and whatever you need for school," she said sternly. "I'm going to wake up that other dummy." She jerked her head in the direction of Cory's room and smiled. I nodded and went to my room to get some clothes. I could hear Cory through our shared wall, very confused about why Grandma was here and why he had to pack.

The front door opened again while I was starting to put some clothes in my book bag. Was Granddad here, too?

"What are you doing here?" Mom's voice. Luke hovering next to her.

"I'm here to get these goddamn kids that you left alone thanks to *this* motherfucker." Grandma was pointing at Luke. Mom pushed her way past Grandma into the apartment.

"Ma, they're fine—I was gone for a minute!" Mom protested.

"Robin, you were gone long enough for me to get dressed, get a cab over here, and get these kids packed. Where the *fuck* were you?" I'd never heard Grandma so mad before. I couldn't tell if her voice was shaking her body or if her body was shaking her voice.

"It's none of your business, Ma, they're fine." Mom walked over to me and grabbed me in a hug as if to prove that everything was okay. She muffled my crying by pushing my face into her stomach.

"And you let that motherfucker drive *my* car? I didn't get that car for him!" Grandma was shouting, spitting. Cory was crying behind his bedroom door; I was crying into Mom's abdomen. Luke was standing in the middle of the living room, glaring at my grandmother.

"Cut it out, Ma, god! We're fine!" Maybe Mom thought that if she kept saying it, it would be true.

Grandma marched up to Mom, her pointer finger leading the way. "Listen to me—I am *done*." Grandma was so quiet now it seemed worse than the yelling. "These kids can have anything they want from me, but you? As long as that motherfucker is in this house? Lose my number, bitch." Grandma kissed me and Cory on the forehead on her way out the door. The cab that was waiting for her took her back over the mountain and out of our lives.

10.

didn't know why we were moving. Mom had worked so hard to fix up our apartment; she sent us away, worked overtime. This apartment was designed around sacrifice, a step up into a new and better life. Now we were just . . . going somewhere else.

Mom tried to make it sound exciting. "The new apartment is bigger!" she said. "And everyone will have their own bedroom."

The new house was still in town, but it was far enough that I now had to take the bus to school. It was a split-level ranch, yellow on top and brick on the bottom. I only knew to describe it that way because I kept reading about Elizabeth and Jessica's house in the Sweet Valley Twins books and, having lived in apartments my whole life, had no idea what the fuck they were describing until I asked Mom. The bottom of the house was closed off to us by a locked door, and we lived in the top part.

Luke stopped visiting me at night for a while. But that didn't last long.

My main memory of the lake house is hunger.

We never seemed to have food anymore. Mom had always monitored what we ate; we had never been allowed to just pig out on snacks or help ourselves to cold cuts. Groceries were expensive, and she was careful about food stamps since they were doled out on a schedule. But we *had* snacks and could count on a regular routine of meals before Luke came to live with us.

Part of the reason we didn't have food is that we also didn't have money. Mom had left her job at Pendine for a better paying job at the hospital; I could hear Mom and Luke fighting about it in their room, Mom asking him what he did with her paycheck, and me wondering why she gave it to him in the first place. We didn't have food stamps anymore because Mom was working so much. Luke's full-time job seemed to be doing whatever it was that made him wide-eyed and sweaty every time he came out of their bedroom after one of his frequent trips to the city.

The school lunch was often my only meal of the day. I lived for sloppy joes and square-cut pizza and felt comforted by the way the food all fit into the molded portions of the plastic tray.

Getting lunch was thrilling, but buying lunch was hard. Cory and I were on the reduced-lunch program at school, and much like the food stamps Mom once used, it was an obvious and slightly embarrassing spectacle every time I approached the cashier. Everyone who ate hot lunch at school had a wallet-size card; you brought it to the cashier, and they punched a hole or stamped one of the boxes for every meal. If your parents paid the full price, you got to put your card back in your pocket, where everyone hoped you wouldn't lose it.

Reduced-lunch cards were kept in an envelope with the cashier. They were a dull, washed-out green instead of the vibrant pink of the full-paying kids. Worst of all, you had to give the cashier your name and hold up the line while she dug through the envelope trying to find it. "Henderson," I said softly, hoping no one behind me would notice. If you were lucky, the kids behind you in line would only whisper about how poor you were. Usually they were much more cruel.

"Oh, she's reduced lunch," they hissed to each other. "That's why it's taking so long."

"Which one?" the cashier said, slightly too loudly.

"Danielle." I didn't have to make the effort to stay quiet this time; I was so embarrassed that my voice disappeared.

The cashier punched my card and put it back in the envelope.

"FINALLY," the kids behind me snickered. My skin felt cold. I couldn't look anyone in the eye as I carried my tray to a table. At eight years old, I already felt the imbalance of a world that never wanted me to forget that I had nothing.

Mom was always at work or in the city with Luke. My go-to

dinner was Old El Paso taco shells. We always seemed to have a box around, even though I never saw Mom make tacos a day in her life. Taco shells are not very filling. They don't taste very good cold. And they definitely didn't taste like Doritos, even though they mimicked the texture. You can't eat them as a sandwich; the minute you pressed the top half-moons together, it was bound to crack at the bottom.

Dry spaghetti sometimes worked in a pinch, too. Blue-box Ronzoni, two sticks at a time. It wasn't smart to chew more than two—dry spaghetti had a tendency to break into tiny sharp pieces that sometimes would lodge in your throat.

Luke always had food. He'd come home with slices of pizza, fast-food burgers, all for himself. I would find a way to be in the kitchen when he was eating, just in case he wanted to offer me a french fry or an entire McDonald's cheeseburger. He never did. He rounded his back and put both of his arms on the table, protectively encircling his plate.

Sometimes Mom would try to get him to give us something. "C'mon, Luke, you can't give them some of your fries?" She'd be standing at the sink, pleading but still cautious, knowing full well that he never wanted to share. Usually he would laugh at her, at us, and keep eating.

But one time he stood up, walked over to her slowly, and smacked her across her face.

I sat at the table staring at Mom as Luke sat down, wiped his mouth with his napkin, and kept eating. Mom caressed her cheek with both hands and cried, silently, her shoulders hiccuping up and down. I got up to see if she was okay. "I'm fine, Dani," she said, sniffing back her tears, pushing me away with her left hand without looking at me.

A cold feeling crept through my body and settled on my skin in a cool sweat as I realized: the person I counted on most in the world was just as powerless as I was.

———

Mom woke me up one night and told me to start packing. "School clothes and books only." She snapped open a couple of black garbage bags and left them in the corner of the room.

"What's happening?" I asked, still groggy from sleep.

"We're moving tomorrow morning."

"Where?"

"Warwick."

"Why?"

"Does it matter, Dani?" Mom was annoyed, frantically putting my clothes into the garbage bags. "C'mon, get your shit."

We were being evicted for not paying rent, but I didn't know that.

"Where are we gonna live? Where am I gonna go to school?" I had a million more questions, but the look on Mom's face indicated that I shouldn't ask any of them.

"We'll be living with your grandma." I hadn't seen my grandma in months. Would she even want to see me?

I stuffed down my tears and made sure my schoolbooks were in my backpack. "What about my toys?"

"We'll come back for them later," she lied.

If I had been given one crucial piece of information in that moment, I would have gone from crying to laughing: Mom and Luke were breaking up, and he had moved to California.

We moved early the next morning, taking a cab over the mountain to Warwick, where we lived in the big room upstairs at Grandma's. Cory and I took the bus to school. Granddad still went to work as a bartender in the city. I loved seeing Grandma so much; she always hugged me tight, and it didn't feel like she loved us any less since the last time we saw her. We watched Mets games together, and I did my homework at the kitchen table after school, loading up on super-sugary 4C iced tea that I made from the giant can of powder in the pantry.

I came home after school one day, and Mom was gone. According to Grandma, she moved to the city to be with Luke.

Of course, a lot more was going on than I knew. Not many parents confide to their children about the ins and outs of their love lives, and even though I was nosy, I was only nine. It turns out Mom had started calling Luke from the pay phone in front of Grand Union; when Grandma discovered this, she kicked Mom out. She was twenty-nine years old and knew something none of us did—she was pregnant. With nowhere to go, she went to the Bronx to live with Luke's mom, and Luke came back from California. They reconciled, and a couple of months later, they came back to Warwick and got an apartment on Cherry Street. Cory and I didn't move in with them right away; Mom said she needed time to get the apartment together, and I was in no hurry to rejoin Luke. But the thought I wouldn't ever be able to shake, the thing that haunted me immediately:

We could have gotten away from him forever, and she brought him back.

———

Mom barely let us unpack before she told us she was pregnant. She was beaming about it. All of the moms on TV and in the movies were always fully pregnant, even if they just found out—their bellies were swollen, filled with the very idea of pregnancy. Mom was still skinny, so I couldn't really tell how she knew there was a baby in there, but then I remembered all of that period stuff. Disgusting. Luke puffed his chest out.

"I'm going to have a son," he said loudly. Mom shushed him, said there was no way he could tell it was going to be a boy. "I can tell," he said, leaning down to yell right at her belly. "You're a boy!" Mom jokingly pushed him away. He kissed her on the cheek as he came up. His wide smile looked demonic to me.

"And that's *my* son," he said, standing up fully. "Not like y'all— y'all don't have a father." He laughed.

"Aw, Luke, don't say that!" Mom said.

"It's true, they don't. And I'm not your father, either." He pointed at Mom. "I'm his father, only."

Mom shook her head but said nothing more.

We only lived on Cherry Street for a few months before we moved again. The house on Ackerman Road was similar to the lake house—a blue split-level ranch. It was on the outskirts of town, farther away from Grandma and surrounded by woods, with so many trees between each house you couldn't see any neighbors.

It had three proper bedrooms; Mom and Luke were in the back corner, Cory was in the other corner, and I had a small room off the hall, across from the bathroom.

The landlords were a nice family that lived farther back on the property. They had an old blue pickup truck that they let Luke and Mom use for errands sometimes, like taking our clothes to the laundromat. They also had two kids, Julia and Reuben, and a huge trampoline and treehouse separated them from our view.

Ackerman Road increased our isolation—I couldn't walk to Grandma's house, get a slice at Frank's Pizza, or access anything that was comforting to me. Mom worked a lot, picking up extra shifts at the hospital before the baby made her too uncomfortable to move around easily. She was tired; most days she would come home from work, sit on the couch, and fall asleep with her mouth wide-open, her head drooping to the side. Luke didn't really work—he stayed in the bedroom, where I could hear the snap of his lighter working for hours after we got home from school. He would eventually emerge—shirtless, his eyes black and consumed by his pupils, a thin sheen of sweat on his forehead. If I tried to say hello or ask how he was doing, he would turn toward me in zombie-like motions, trying to register the origin of the interruption. He was smoking crack or snorting cocaine almost all day, but to me, he was just acting stranger than usual.

Anything we did now was met with Luke's fist.

I don't even remember what set him off this particular night, only that I had walked into the living room. Did I say something to him? Walk with too heavy a footstep? Make too much noise?

Ask to watch something on TV? Whatever it was, he was off the couch and slamming me down the hallway before I knew it. He picked me up by my neck, which he had never done before, and slid my body up the wall near the steps. His breath was hot; he was panting, and each time he exhaled, spit hit my face.

He dropped me to the floor, where I collapsed in a pile of sobs, trying to make myself as small as possible. It didn't matter: he was bigger and stronger than me. He grabbed my arm, twisted it back, and shoved me down the hall. I didn't feel the underside of my middle toe slicing against the hinge of the closet near my bedroom, right at the base, where the toes meet the fleshy part of the foot. I only realized I was hurt when Luke yelled about the blood I was getting everywhere.

What I do remember is that my mom was there and watched the whole thing from the couch.

She scooped me up and took me to the bathroom. She made me sit on the lid of the toilet, while she sat on the edge of the tub with my foot on her knee. Every time she touched my toe, I screamed.

"I have to see how bad the cut is, Dani! Calm down!"

She gently bent my toe back, and a shock of pain shot up my foot. I screamed again, tears pouring out of me like a faucet.

"All right," Mom said, annoyed. "We have to go to the hospital."

She left me in the bathroom with a towel while she went to borrow the landlord's pickup truck. When she came back into the house to get me, propping me against her on my uninjured side so that I could hop down the steps, Luke asked where we were going.

"I'm taking her to the hospital," Mom hissed. I hadn't heard her take this tone with him in a while. She was pissed.

"For that little cut?" Luke said, looking right at me.

"She needs stitches."

Mom helped me down the stairs into the pickup, which she had left running. As we drove down the dark road, I stepped on the towel to keep it pressed against my foot. "It was just an accident," she said, her eyes fixed on the road. "That's all. Because they're going to ask what happened. So you tell them the truth—that it was an accident." I was scared by the amount of blood soaking through the towel, but I was terrified by Mom asking me to lie.

When the nurse finally called us, she helped me over to a cot. "Let's get this cleaned up a little, okay?"

Mom said, "Kids, right? So clumsy. Especially this one." She laughed a little, in a mother's-work-is-never-done sort of way, gesturing toward me and shaking her head.

The nurse pulled up a little stool and sat at the end of the cot, her face close to my toe. When she was done, I lifted my foot to check it out. It didn't look like anything had happened from the front. But when I bent my foot over my knee, I was able to see the thick, wiry stitches sticking out like the bristles on a hairbrush.

"Keep a Band-Aid on it until we get her in for a checkup," the nurse said to Mom.

But we never would come back. Luke said it was a waste of money, and Mom didn't protest. A few weeks later, after it looked pretty well healed, I used the scissors Mom kept in the bathroom cabinet to snip the knots and pull the threads out myself.

"You and Cory are having dinner with Julia and Reuben tonight."

I started to protest but stopped myself. It was a Saturday; Mom was working nights at the hospital, which meant Luke was responsible for dinner, which meant we probably wouldn't eat. I was pretty sure that Julia was a weirdo, but at least they had food. "Okay."

"Wear clean clothes," Mom said as she left for work. I didn't even know if I had clean clothes.

I walked into my bedroom. I didn't have any furniture aside from the bed; a few things were on hangers, but most of my clothes were scattered on the floor of the closet in loose piles. The overhead light was the only one in the room. I flipped the switch and started digging through the mess. I missed having a dresser. My face started to feel hot, already anticipating the embarrassment I would feel when I showed up to dinner wearing a sweatshirt that smelled like last week's lunch. I pulled a white-and-green horizontal-striped knit sweater out of the pile. There was a ketchup stain near the neck from where someone jokingly threw a fish stick at me during lunch. It was funny at the time, even though the lunch monitor yelled at us. Looking at the dried-up crust of ketchup now just made me feel like I was a loser.

I knew how to hand-wash a stain, but all I had was the bar of Ivory soap that every single person in the house used to wash their bodies. I turned on the tap for a few seconds, just long enough to get the fabric wet without it being soaked. I started rubbing the soap on the ketchup stain, pushing into the knits and purls, hoping Ivory was just as good as proper laundry detergent. The stain turned from red to light pink, then, after a few more minutes of scrubbing, looked like it was almost gone. The corner of the bar of soap was worn, reminding me of a corner you might fold to keep your place in a book.

I didn't account for the sweater absorbing so much water, though. The top half was completely soaked. The whole sweater sagged as I held it up to wring it out, twisting out as much water as I could. When I unfurled it and held it up again, it was still wet and now deeply wrinkled.

We didn't own a hair dryer. Every white friend I knew had one standard issue; girls were starting to talk in homeroom about how hard it was to dry their hair in the winter mornings and how sometimes it would freeze into hard strands. Mom used to do my hair in complicated braids and styles; now she would just tell me to wash it every once in a while, make sure I combed through it, and let my pillow suck all of the extra wetness out of it while I slept.

I took the sweater back to my room and locked the door. I put my undershirt on quickly, scared Luke would ask for a massage while I was getting dressed for dinner. He mostly came into my room at night, when everyone was sleeping, to press and rub against me, but lately he had started asking me to give him massages during the day. He'd call to me from the bedroom, where he spent most of his time.

"Dani. Dani, come here."

I would crank their bedroom door open slowly. Bedsheets hung in the windows in place of curtains, making the unmade bed and clothes-strewn closet muted, even in the middle of the day. If he wasn't already facedown on the mattress when he called to me, he made a big show of turning over, groaning and stretching and pushing the sheet aside.

"Come rub my back."

He made me sit on his front once, but looking at his face while I sat on his naked body made me so nervous I shook uncontrollably, so he never made me do it that way again. Usually he made me straddle his butt, sometimes reaching back to push my knees against his hips so that I wouldn't fully sit up when I tried to reach the top of his back. I didn't know how to give a proper massage, and I was afraid to make him angry.

"What should I do?"

"Just press your hand here and rub it in a circle," Luke said, pointing to a spot on his shoulder or lower back. His groans made me feel like there were rocks dropping into my stomach the way we dropped rocks into the river on the footbridge in Stanley-Deming Park. I didn't want to press too hard; if I hurt him, he would hit me for sure. Making him happy was even worse.

"Push harder. Yeah, like that." He always asked me to push hard enough that I had to rock against him. Sometimes he moved one hand underneath him while I gave him a massage; the way he moved it made me think he was rubbing his belly the way Mom used to rub mine when I had a stomachache. Luke would groan really loud, his hand not moving but still underneath him, and I'd rub his back until I heard him snore, finally feeling safe enough to leave.

Now I needed to keep him away while I got ready, but I was nervous about the lock; if he tried to come in and wasn't able to, he might smack me in the face like last time, when I wanted to do my homework without Cory interrupting, so I pushed the button on the door handle to keep him out. Only it wasn't Cory trying to get in while I was going over my vocabulary words. He pushed the handle, then said, "Dani, open this door." I scrambled from my bed and opened it. I tried to apologize, but his palm was against my temple before I finished the "I" in "I'm sorry." I thought that only cartoon characters saw stars, like when Wile E. Coyote fell off a cliff, but when my head bounced off the wall with the force of his slap, white dots appeared everywhere. It was like I was looking through gauze, even though my eyes were wide-open.

"You don't lock the door unless I tell you to lock the door," he said, walking into the bathroom.

I had felt funny for the rest of the day after that smack, like I was floating in a lake, hearing everything from just under the surface of the water. I didn't want to show up to dinner with the landlords feeling that hazy. I put my wet sweater on over my undershirt and quickly unlocked the door.

I was excited to see the inside of the landlords' house, but we didn't get farther than the kitchen. The parents had us sit at the small round table to the left of the main door they used to enter the house.

We were already sitting at the table when Reuben came downstairs. His short brown hair was slicked against his forehead with sweat; his pallor was chalky, and dark circles ringed his eyes. As he hunched and shuffled over to the table, his mom pulled out a chair for him.

"Hi, I'm Danielle."

"Hi," he said, without meeting my gaze. He was moving the food around with his fork. Mom had told us that Reuben had just had some major surgery, so I tried to take the pressure off and talk to Julia and her parents instead.

About two minutes after he sat down, Reuben let out a loud growl. I put down my fork and looked at him. He had his arms wrapped around his tummy, and his head was dropping toward his lap. He groaned again, and this time it morphed into a scream as he raised his head and bent his body over the chair backward. It looked like something out of *The Exorcist*, which of course I had seen because I had no proper supervision in my life.

Reuben's mom jumped up and stood behind him, but he was up and moving. Hunched, he swiveled around, almost running right into his mom, who grabbed him by the shoulders. "Do you need your medicine?" Reuben said no and ran to his room. She grabbed a bottle of pills from the kitchen counter and followed him in.

I felt bad for Reuben, but I also couldn't shake the other thing I was feeling: pure jealousy. I definitely didn't want whatever he had. But his mom was so nice and attentive and loving. They had dinner at a table and a trampoline to jump on. They were safe. They were loved.

I couldn't remember the last time I felt that way.

When Mom had the baby, they named him after his dad. They called him Little Luke. I hated that name. I called him the Baby.

He was cute, all round cheeks and black eyes. He made funny sounds, and he liked to look around, even though Mom told me he couldn't see anything yet. Luke was supposed to be taking care of the Baby now that Mom worked nights as a nurse's aide, but he frequently left us alone, preferring instead to drive to the city. When he took off, I did it instead.

I got pretty good at feeding him. I watched Mom while she prepared his bottles, eager for any time I got to spend with her, even if I was just shadowing her in the kitchen. Sometimes she'd make a joke, the old Mom I used to know peeking her head out around the shadow of the tired, sigh-filled woman she was now. Most of the time she just talked to herself in a low whisper, as if she was checking things off a list she compiled in her head. I watched, so that I could help. If I helped enough, maybe the old version of Mom would stick around longer, until she was back to being the kind of woman who would swing branches to protect me.

I carried the Baby to the kitchen and ticked the steps off in my head, working with one hand while I bounced the Baby on my shoulder with the other. Rinse out a bottle. Put in the powdered formula with the scoop already in the container, just one. Carry it to the sink. Put in some water. Shake shake shake. Put it back on the counter. Grab a small pot. Fill it with water. Put it on the stove, now that I was allowed to use it out of necessity. Turn the dial and watch the flames roar to life. Turn it down—you don't want it boiling, just warm. Watch the water and rock the baby. Put the bottle in, only for a couple of minutes. Take it out. Hold the Baby and the bottle in the same hand; squirt some on your wrist. Walk to the couch, sit down, hold the Baby in your lap. Keep his head up a little. Feed him. Take the bottle out of his mouth every minute or so—he has to breathe. Put him back on your shoulder. Bounce him and pat his back until he burps. Tickle his little belly for a few minutes, because making him laugh makes you happy. Check his diaper. Change his diaper, but don't forget to wipe his testicles, because sometimes he shits so much it goes up his back and all over his front. Wrap the diaper into a small package, cinch it closed with the sticky tabs on the side. Put him back in his crib. Sit with him in the dark, until he sounds like he's sleeping. Check the Timex alarm clock next to Mom's side of the bed, and note the time: 4:00 a.m. Grab the diaper. Creep out of the bedroom like a cat burglar. Say a secular prayer—please, please don't wake up again until Mom comes home. Please. Throw out the diaper in the kitchen. Crawl back into your bed. Stare at the ceiling.

I was ten years old.

I wasn't sleeping a lot. New sisterhood was exhausting.

It surprised me how much Luke loved the Baby. "My *son*," he would say, lifting the Baby out of his crib and holding him up so high he almost touched his back to the ceiling. "I *love you*." Things evened out a little with the Baby around. Luke still hit me, still emerged from the bedroom wide-eyed, sweating, and looking for violence. But the Baby made him happier. He liked seeing a little version of himself walking around in the world. His childish sense of humor matched well with an audience that couldn't even use its neck muscles yet.

I was nervous every time he held the Baby, knowing intimately how quickly his moods shifted. But he never showed an ounce of his evil to the Baby. I assumed he hated all children, but it turns out he was selective.

When the Baby was just a few months old, Luke announced that Davon was coming to live with us.

"Who's that?" He said it so matter-of-factly, but I'd never heard that name before.

"My son."

"Where does he live?"

"In the Bronx, with his whore mother. But he wants to come stay here, so I'm gonna go get him."

I had no idea Luke had another kid. I looked at Mom.

"You know—Davon!" She acted like if she said it loud enough I'd suddenly remember something I'd never been told. Where were we even going to put another kid? I felt sick. Luke was adding to his team, and soon I'd be outnumbered.

Davon was seven years old. He had a broad face and tiny body. The Baby was the spitting image of Luke; Davon must have looked like his mother. Mom and Luke put a mattress on the floor in Cory's room, which he was now going to share. "It's not fair," Cory whispered to me in the hallway as we went to our rooms. He didn't like the arrangement at all but knew there was nothing he could do about it. Luke was not someone who debated.

Davon was rambunctious in the way that all seven-year-olds are, testing boundaries by saying no and wearing his defiance like a second skin. He was loud. Wild. He needed too much attention in a house where there was already so little to spare. His transition to the country life must have been disorienting, but I didn't think about that. He annoyed me instantly, leaving little room for sympathy.

He had only been there for a few weeks when it happened. The day was otherwise unremarkable—I woke up hungry, went to school hateful, and came home scared. Luke was home, sniffing and wild-eyed. Mom was at work. The school must have called while Cory and I were on the bus, not knowing that an unhinged beast would answer.

When Davon got off his bus and came into the house, Luke grabbed him and shouted, "Did you push someone at school?" Davon protested; Luke smacked him for lying. "Get in there." Davon was already crying from the smack as Luke pushed him into Cory's bedroom. I will never forget the way he held his hand to his face, his mouth open but soundless, tears streaming over his pinky finger as he walked into the room. I ran to my room, which shared a wall, and heard every sound of what came next.

To say that Luke beat Davon mercilessly is an understatement. I knew what it was like to be hit, I knew what it felt to be terrorized. But he never beat me so badly that my blood left dripping stains on the sink. He never kicked while I scrambled to the bathroom, ran to find a way out, leaving finger trails of blood where I tried to grasp the door, the knob, the floor, anything. Making it to the bathroom only to have Luke follow with an extension cord and whipping, punching, kicking.

I listened to Davon scream in the bathroom, right across the hall. I moved to the floor near my closet and pulled my knees up to my chin. He might come for me next. I crawled into the closet and hid, wishing I could push myself through the wall and disappear.

After, Davon was quiet. Possibly unconscious. I was too afraid to come out of my room to check on him. I eventually heard Luke send Davon to bed. I stayed in my room all night, listening through the wall as Cory tried to console Davon while he wept.

The next day, he sent us all to school. Cory left for school before

I did, and Davon's bus was later than mine, so we didn't see each other. I was numb, terrified by the notion that Luke's viciousness could be the new normal.

The cops showed up shortly after Cory and I got off the bus at the end of the day. Mom was home, finally, and opened the front door when they knocked. When I came around the corner and down the stairs to stand next to her, she was crying. She hugged me against her while she talked to the cops. Of course she hadn't known. She had just gotten home herself. Yes, she worked nights. I heard fragments of the conversation as they walked Davon out of the house to the ambulance.

Any other children in the home. Can't be allowed within one thousand feet of the two older children. No, never again. Arrested. His teacher called Child Protective Services. Firearms. Child's mother lives in the Bronx. Drugs, both of them? Both of them. What kind? Cocaine. Heroin. Crack. Not sure about her. Okay. And you? Never. Nothing ever? Okay. Court date. Jail. Bail.

I was transfixed by the blue and red lights bouncing off the tree trunks, small dots of light piercing through the trees and catching on Julia's trampoline. When Luke was brought out of the house, his eyes were wide, but he walked with an easy calmness, his arms handcuffed behind his back. He was biting his lip when they pushed his head down and lowered him into the police car. I pulled away from Mom as she went inside the house but waited outside until the police cars and ambulance left.

I needed to see it for myself.

That he was really gone.

11.

"Ugh. None of this is even clean. Who even lives like this? Animals."

Grandma was sitting on a chair in her kitchen, giant black garbage bags full of our clothes surrounding her. Outside the windows the sky was black, and owls were hooting from the barn. We'd already been at this for hours.

One of the garbage bags was split open between Grandma's knees; she straddled it as she pulled out our clothes. In the stark overhead light of her clean kitchen, everything looked positively filthy.

"God, I just bought this for you! Already stained." Grandma was throwing clothes around the kitchen on hyperspeed, upset by everything she touched. The ash of her cigarette was inches long; she was so mad, she forgot to smoke.

"When is Mom coming back?" I asked.

Grandma silently dug into the next garbage bag.

Mom must have taken time off work after Davon's beating, because she was home with the Baby for a couple of days. We didn't talk about what happened. Cory and I would ask about Davon, and whether he was coming back; Mom would wearily reply, "I don't know." I tried to hold on to the feeling of Luke not being around—I felt lighter, less scared, less anxious. But the good feeling was always punctured by reality. He would come back, one day.

A few days after the incident, Mom took Cory and me to Grandma's house for the weekend. I didn't know it at the time, but she was going to bail Luke out, and he couldn't legally be near us until the child abuse case with Davon was settled. "I'm taking the baby to the Bronx to see his other grandma," she said, lugging my book bag out of the back seat of the landlord's truck. "I'll be back soon."

Our parting was rushed and unceremonious—not even a mild tremor to indicate the tectonic shift that was happening as I rushed into Grandma's house, thinking only of pizza and Monopoly. I didn't want to be near Mom; I was furious that she was going to the city. Going with him. But I couldn't bear her leaving us. I had spent the last three years missing her, even when we were in the same room. Now she was leaving to take care of Luke. It felt like too much, even for a weekend. I was living in a crevasse, pressed between anger and fear.

A month later, the anger gave way completely to the fear. She hadn't even called. What if she never came back?

"I don't know when she's coming back, Dani," Grandma said sharply. "And if I see that motherfucking asshole any time soon, I'm going to fucking kill her." She was never one to modulate her language around us, but whenever Mom's name came up now, Grandma launched into a string of expletives so intense I could go to the kitchen, pour a cup of iced tea, and come back before she was finished.

Now Grandma stopped throwing clothes into piles and stubbed out her cigarette in the ashtray on the kitchen table. "Come here," she said, holding out her arms. I jumped over a jumbled pile of my sweaters and underwear and stood in front of her. She grabbed me into a hug and kissed my cheek, hard.

"I love you," she said, her voice shaky. "Grandma's never going to leave you again, okay, honeychild?"

When I pulled back from her to nod, she was lifting her glasses with one hand to wipe under her eyes with the other.

"All right," she sighed. "We have to go clothes shopping. Let's just see what we can save here and take it to the laundromat tomorrow. Help me sort these. Whites and colors."

I'd never sorted laundry before. As I got to work, something was starting to sink in. "So if all our clothes are here . . . are we staying here?"

"I don't know, child."

I would never live with Mom again.

When Grandma and Granddad retired to Warwick, they rented a two-bedroom duplex. They might have kept their house in Greenwood Lake if they thought they would be raising kids again. I was allowed to lock my door here, but there was no need for it. Besides, none of the locks worked anyway. The town was safe, the apartment was safe—no one even locked the front door. It would take years for me to adjust to the idea that no one was coming for me in the night.

The living room had bloodred wall-to-wall carpeting and wood-paneled walls, giving it a simultaneously horrifying and old-fashioned feeling, like you were always about to get murdered in a 1970s John Carpenter movie. Grandma hung heavy cream-colored drapes in the living room; during the day, the sunlight and hanging veil of cigarette smoke gave the whole room a Victorian effect, complemented by the walled-over and painted fireplace against the wall shared with the kitchen. Grandma and Granddad went to Sears in Middletown and bought a new couch when they moved; the new one was dark, with navy and maroon stripes running down the cushions. The same two stylish wooden end tables we had in Greenwood Lake flanked each side, with the same ornate lamps. The only two books in the house sat on one of the end tables: a Bible with a faux leather cover that Grandma used to prop up her hand when she was painting her nails and a first-edition copy of *Roots* that Sweetie Pie inscribed for Cory when he was born, hastily scrawling my name under his when I was born a year later. Everything in the house screamed ELDERLY PEOPLE LIVE HERE, from the gold curtain sashes to the twenty-year-old Tupperware. I'd never noticed how old my grandparents were until I was around them every day.

Both of the bedrooms were upstairs—I shared the bigger one with Grandma, and Cory shared with Granddad. There were already twin beds in the small room, carried over the mountain from Greenwood Lake. I slept with Grandma in her big bed for a couple of months, until she could afford two twin beds for our room. She usually fell asleep on the couch watching TV, so I had the whole thing to myself. I liked to stretch my legs as far as I could, pushing my toes toward the cooler parts of the sheet.

"So you and Granddad won't sleep in the same bed anymore?"

"Believe me—we've slept next to each other long enough," Grandma said, rolling her eyes.

"But you won't even be in the same room. Husbands and wives are supposed to sleep together."

I'd watched enough TV to have this whole marriage thing figured out.

"Go ahead, keep telling me about what husbands and wives are supposed to do. You wanna sleep in the barn? Be my guest." Grandma tilted her head toward the back of the house and raised her eyebrows.

The barn was a relic lost to time, not important enough to refurbish but too cumbersome to tear down. It was about thirty feet away from the back of the house and was mostly a haven for wild animals, namely skunks, possums, and raccoons. During the summer, I constantly woke up with the fresh-baked stench of skunk spray wafting into our open windows.

We fell into something that resembled normalcy. We got by with Granddad's bartending and gambling job and Grandma's Sears card. I did my homework at the kitchen table after school, sneaking slices of salami out of the refrigerator while Grandma sat in the living room watching TV. The rustling of the plastic bag always gave me away, no matter how quiet I tried to be.

"You're going to ruin your appetite!" Grandma shouted one day as I slipped a thin slice between my fingers. "And stop eating it plain—it's for sandwiches."

But I couldn't help it. It had been a while since we had food available whenever we were hungry.

"Where's your brother?" Grandma asked.

"I don't know. Probably outside with Chucky and Justin." Chucky and Justin were neighborhood kids; they were exactly Cory's age and shared his general disregard for common decency. Cory had developed an after-school routine of his own that largely involved keying cars, riding his bike into oncoming traffic, and other acts of minor delinquency. His life was outside—I rarely saw him, and when I did, we still fought like demons. He kept having fun, as if everything with Mom and Luke didn't even happen. I didn't know how to talk to him. Other siblings may have banded together or grown closer in such a traumatic environment, but we became two islands, connected by nothing, sharing only the violent waves beating at our shore.

Even though the middle school was less than a mile away, everyone took the bus. Warwick was a wealthy village, with the majority of families living in large split-level homes on the outskirts of town; the lack of sidewalks and distance meant most kids couldn't walk to school even if they wanted to, so we townies got to take the bus by default, a consolation prize meant to make us feel included.

Grandma woke us up for school every day by slamming into our bedrooms, turning on the overhead lights, and saying, "Get your ass up—I'm not coming in here again." Cory went to school earlier than me, but I got up anyway, knowing there wouldn't be another alarm.

I first met Angela at the bus stop, on the corner right in front of the tire store. I could tell she was cool from the second I saw her. She had big blond curls bouncing against her olive skin, and bright green eyes. She looked like an exotic flower, even wrapped up in her little-kid uniform of a bright, puffy coat. Most importantly, I noticed her L.A. Gear sneakers right away. Poor kids have a way of zooming in on name brands, mesmerized by their inaccessibility.

"Hi. I'm Angela. What grade are you in?" She spoke with the confidence of someone who didn't care whether we became friends.

"Fourth grade."

"Me too. Who's your teacher?"

"Ms. Post?"

"I have Mr. Terrell. Ms. Post is tall like you."

Our school bus rounded the corner. I turned my head both ways before crossing. When I looked up again, Angela was already halfway across the street. She crossed without even checking to see if a car was about to veer around the bus and smash into her. I couldn't tell if it was the coolest or dumbest thing I'd ever seen.

We sat together on the bus and trudged up the staircase to the top floor, the fourth-grade floor, together. Angela seemed to know everyone, saying hello to most of the girls and sneering at most of the boys. I had only been at this school for a couple of months; we mostly hung out with our class, so there wasn't much overlap with the other kids. Angela hovered in the doorway of one room and pointed next door to another. "That's your class, in there," she said. "See you at recess." I didn't tell her that I already knew where my classroom was, that I was only new to Smith Street, not Warwick. She would become a new friend, someone I could hang out with at home. It felt like the first normal thing that had happened since Mom left.

A few months after we arrived, Uncle Bobby moved in. After two years in California with Aunt Rene, she was sending him home.

"But why is he coming here?" Grandma and I were cleaning out the walk-in closet at the top of the stairs. I was in the process of dragging a set of old, light blue leather suitcases into the hall when I asked the question that had been bugging me the most.

"Where the fuck else is he going to go, Dani? Put that little one inside the big one. Save space." Grandma was hanging a new set of curtains above the singular window. We couldn't move without bumping into each other.

"Is he going to have any room?" I was pissed—why had I never been offered this closet space? He wasn't even here yet, and he already had the best room.

"He's going to have whatever space he has," Grandma said. She finished hanging the curtains and climbed down from the small wooden stool. "Let's get the bed."

I zipped up the suitcase-within-a-suitcase and dragged the whole shebang over to a corner. Grandma was already in the hall, walking the twin mattress from side to side, edging it closer to the door an inch at a time. We had so many twin mattresses in our house by then I wondered if Sears gave my grandparents some kind of punch card.

By the time Bobby arrived, his room had a small TV, a lamp, and an end table/nightstand that he could put some clothes in. He seemed like the same guy he was in California—short-tempered and instantly resentful of my presence. He sat in his room most of the day and chain-smoked. He didn't seem to be interested in finding a job, which is apparently why Aunt Rene told him he had to leave in the first place. I try now to imagine being twenty-seven, aimless, living with my parents and two tweenagers. Smoking myself to death in a tiny locked room would seem like a fine alternative to me, too.

Uncle Bobby didn't like me, but I couldn't stand him, either. Our unconventional living situation had worked for the four of us. The addition of another person made it suddenly feel strained, pushed past the capacity of what we could all endure. Plus, he was a complete weirdo.

Uncle Bobby talked to himself all the time. It wasn't the same as the loud way Grandma ran down a list of stuff she needed to buy from the Grand Union while looking in the refrigerator—Uncle Bobby talked to himself in a stage whisper, which upped the creep factor considerably. I would be in my room doing homework on my bed, and his door would open. A fog of smoke would drift out, like he had just ended a cracking set at Madison Square Garden and was coming back for an encore. He'd run down the stairs, whispering like he was in full conversation with someone. I could only hear the sibilant S's and, once he reached the bottom of the stairs, the occasional laugh.

The laugh freaked me out more than the whisper-talk. Was he laughing at his own jokes? Laughing at an unheard part of a conversation with someone in his head? Both answers were deeply unsettling.

I mostly resented Uncle Bobby for being able to live a life I could only dream of. Even at ten years old, I had chores and homework and responsibilities. He, on the other hand, waited until everyone left the house, came downstairs, popped the *Carrie* tape into the VCR, and watched his favorite movie all day long while he chain-smoked and ate us out of house and home. He was a grown-up version of Kevin from *Home Alone*, if his parents had died on the plane and he was living off the insurance.

He inherited Grandma's love of horror movies. Even if he'd seen the same movie a hundred times, he got angry with me and Cory for interrupting. One day we came home from school, rowdy and yelling with the freedom of people who had just spent an entire day being told to shut up. *Swamp Thing* was playing on the TV when we barreled into the house, throwing our book bags in the corner. I ran to the fridge for a tall glass of sugar-laden iced tea and started fighting with Cory—he got there first, and there wasn't enough left in the pitcher for two glasses.

"Will you two shut up? I'm trying to watch something!" Bobby yelled from the living room.

"You've already seen it a million times!" I wasn't about to let desire supersede logic. "Cory, save some for me!"

"You can just make more!" Cory was also a student of logic. Touché, asshole.

"It won't be cold like it is in the fridge!"

"You two! Shut up! For Christ's sake!" Bobby was in the doorway now. The kitchen was filled with a cacophony of screams, all of us working from different scripts.

"Where are my Ding Dongs!" I gave up on the iced tea, looking instead for the box of Hostess goodies I conned Grandma into letting me buy if I went to the Grand Union for milk.

"Oh, I ate those," Bobby said nonchalantly, taking a drag from his cigarette and sitting back down on the couch.

"Those were MINE! I hate you!"

"I don't really like you, either," he said as I stomped by, grabbing my bag and heading up to my room. "Don't you eat at school? Do you have a tapeworm?"

This was his go-to insult whenever he saw me eating. I had to look up "tapeworms" in our set of World Book encyclopedias; once I knew what they were, I started to worry that I really *did* have one. I was always hungry and never seemed to gain any weight. I was also five-ten by the time I was twelve, but the transition of energy being used to increase my height was lost on me. Uncle Bobby had planted the tapeworm seed, so that became the most likely possibility in my increasingly anxious brain.

The truth is that fighting with Uncle Bobby was weirdly

comforting. I knew that I could lash out at him without being hit—kids annoyed him, but Bobby moved through the world gently. Grandma got angry at us, but we were too tall and she was too tired to hit us, even though she sometimes threatened us that she still could if she really wanted to. For the first time in three years, I didn't need the fear that pinballed throughout my body while I lived with Mom and Luke. It didn't disappear, though; it seemed to have transformed into anxiety. I was afraid of the dark and slept with the curtains in my room pulled back so that the streetlight could illuminate my room. I didn't like getting changed for gym; any attention or comments about bodies made me feel like my stomach was taking a private trip on a sinking ship.

I was also furious, at nothing in particular, every day.

"I don't have a tapeworm!" I screamed from the balcony. I couldn't help the tears springing to my eyes; I was living with a parasite that he put there with his thoughts.

"Yeah, you do. Don't be a crybaby about it."

I slammed myself down on the bed, fuming, happy to have such a deserving target for my rage.

12.

Why do you call it a 'book bag'?" Meg Linkh was staring at me with her ice-blue eyes, her nose wrinkled in confusion. "It's a tote bag."

I'd always called the thing I used to carry my schoolbooks around in a book bag, which seemed logical. I didn't have a good answer for Meg.

"I don't know. That's just what we called it at home," I said, flinching a little at the realization that "home" wasn't the right word anymore.

"Well, it's a tote bag," Meg said, smiling. We had become friends in elementary school when I was staying with Grandma, and we shared a love of baseball. Grandma would stop anything for base-ball, and we watched countless Mets games in the summers before Cory and I moved in permanently. My love for it developed along-side my love for spending time with her.

Warwick was a lot like Greenwood Lake in one particular way: I was the only Black kid in my class. The interrogation I used to get about not having a father now became a grilling about living with my grandparents in an apartment. These were the kinds of facts that I leaked out on the playground or when we did assign-ments in groups.

"Where's Smith Street?"

"Why do you live with your grandparents?"

"Why is your hair like that?"

"You don't have a washer and dryer at home?"

Every time I was asked to account for the weirdness of my fam-ily life, I felt shame creeping in like a drop of water on the edge of a page. I couldn't tell them the truth—no one knew about Mom and Luke, and I wanted to keep it that way. Instead, my answer was always the same: I don't know, I don't know, I don't know.

You couldn't exactly call the street we lived on a neighborhood, with its three houses, the cable building, and a laundromat, but the backyard butted up against a street that had more kids living on it. Cory had his friends Chucky and Justin. Angela was Justin's sister; ours was a friendship of convenience, and a total disaster.

We were inseparable for a year after we met at the bus stop. The first time I went to her apartment, I saw how much she looked like her mom, the same bright eyes and curly hair, though Mrs. Allen's hair was jet-black. "My mom is Italian and my dad is Black," Angela said matter-of-factly one day, while we were listening to her Minnie Mouse record and playing with her dolls. I was surprised, and momentarily excited, but then I looked at her. We might have had an element of Blackness in common, but I already knew the world would never treat us the same.

Their apartment was huge and seemed to take up the entire floor of the building. Angela shared a bedroom with her younger sister, Anita, but it was big enough to split equitably. "Who's your dad?"

"I don't know. But he's Black too."

"Where's your mom?" She clanked two doll heads together, making their hair shimmy.

"The city."

"Why don't you live with her in the city?"

"I don't know. We just don't."

She was always incredibly direct, which was both frightening and exhilarating to me. Angela wasn't a bad kid, but she *was* a badass—no one seemed to pick on her, and she always had a comeback if anyone attempted it. One day she came to the bus stop, her teeth bared like an animal ready to strike.

"Look at my caps."

I tilted my head closer, and sure enough, Angela had gold caps on two of her teeth.

"What are those?"

"I just told you—gold caps. I got them in the city."

The only other person I'd seen with gold caps was Slick Rick, in a rap video on MTV. For Angela to saunter through our cow town with the same swagger as a rapper on TV instantly cemented her cool factor forever. She legitimately didn't give a shit what anyone thought of her; Angela lived on a plane of existence so far above the rest of us that we couldn't even come close to touching her.

"That little fast-ass girl is trouble," Grandma said whenever I mentioned Angela, which was constantly. "I saw her at the bus stop one morning in high heels and a miniskirt. In fourth grade!" Grandma was incensed. "Don't you dare try to imitate her—what's really cool is doing your own thing."

I rolled my eyes at her after-school-special logic. Grandma wore polyester pants with elastic waistbands and Cosby sweaters—what the fuck did she know about what was cool?

Angela also changed her mind about people for no discernible reason. "I don't like Amy anymore," she said on the way to school one morning. Amy was kind; she was tall like me, played piano, and had a sick mullet to match Meg, her best friend.

"Why not?"

"I don't know. She's just annoying. Don't sit with her at lunch anymore, okay?"

I didn't know what to say. I liked Amy—she was very funny and really smart. We wrote a book of limericks for a contest, complete with our own illustrations, and we won; our book was "published," just one slim copy in a hard red cover, with both of our names on the spine. For years we shared ownership and traded it back and forth. But I was scared of not having Angela on my side.

I had maintained my friendship with Amy since we were both in Ms. Post's class, but I didn't talk about her anymore. Every time someone passed by the classroom door while I was talking to Amy and Meg, I was terrified it would be Angela on the way to the bathroom. That she would see me laughing with Amy when we partnered up to review our vocabulary words.

Angela started hanging out with two new girls, Laurie and Jackie, when we started sixth grade. They weren't related but may as well have been. They were either from Long Island or the city, earning them instant cool points from everyone—including Angela. We were all starting to experiment with hairspray, but they had already mastered the twelve-inch-high wall of bangs every girl in town was aching to achieve. Both wore thick black eyeliner and bright-colored lipstick. At twelve years old, Laurie and Jackie looked like they had walked right out of a Poison video and into Warwick Valley Middle School.

I didn't like Laurie or Jackie. There were rumors that they filled the handles of their hairbrushes with alcohol instead of hairspray, and they hung out with high school boys. They never did their homework and acted up in class a lot. Angela was a different person around them; she was tougher and laughed only when they were all in their tight cluster, making fun of someone. She and I didn't start out having a lot in common, but now we were hanging on by a thread.

We didn't really hang out at her apartment anymore, but sometimes Angela would deign to grace us with her presence for the odd kickball game in the backyard once the spring weather was nice. She showed up with Justin one day as Chucky, Cory, and I were setting up the rocks and sticks that would constitute the bases.

"I'm pitcher," Angela said, walking to the mound. Pitching was the most coveted position in kickball. The pitcher was the de facto captain of the field, and I wanted just once to taste that kind of power. I asked all the time and the guys always said no; until Angela, it hadn't even occurred to me that I could just walk to the mound and declare it for myself.

I started to argue, but Cory and Chucky told me to shut up. I wanted to play more than I wanted to kick them in the nuts, so I did. The game started normally—kick, run, tagged out, technical home run because someone kicked it into Chucky's backyard. Then, when it was my turn to kick, Angela started changing the rules.

"If you kick it past the barn that's an automatic home run," she said, tossing the soccer ball from hand to hand.

"No way!" I shouted. The barn was so close it may as well have been a base. And who the fuck did she think she was changing the rules mid-game? Without basic decorum and long-standing rules we might as well be those kids from *The Lord of the Flies*. "You can't just change the rules in the middle of the game!"

"No, that's good," Cory said, like the traitor he was. All of the guys could kick it over the barn, so this new rule worked in their favor.

"Okay, that's the rule," Angela said, leaning forward and teeing up for a pitch.

To this day, when I get angry, it feels like a dozen bees are buzzing just under the skin on my forehead. That day, it felt like the whole colony was doing a rhumba. As I stormed to the mound, Angela stood up straight. The guys groaned.

"Come on, we want to play!"

I stopped inches short from her face. "You cannot change the rules!" I was shouting about the game but feeling every devastating emotion I'd had since she casually tossed me aside for the two derelict Long Islanders who were now her best friends. I was mad at her, specifically and in general, for thinking I didn't matter.

Angela laughed.

I didn't plan to punch her in the face. But before I knew it, my hand was a tight ball of rage, making contact with her nose. Her head snapped back. All of the guys shouted, "Oooooooooh," their hands held over their mouths in disbelief. When Angela brought her head back to center, there was a thick, oozing line of maroon dripping out of one nostril.

I burst into tears.

I ran away, down the short pathway on the side of the house, and slammed through the front door. Grandma was sitting in the living room on a kitchen chair, playing *Super Mario Bros.* In theory, the Nintendo was a gift for Cory and me, but Grandma racked up more hours on *The Legend of Zelda*, *Marble Madness*, and *Duck Hunt* than Cory and I could collectively match in a lifetime. I heard the wah-wah sound of Mario dying on the TV as I stood in the foyer weeping.

"Goddammit, I just died," Grandma said, turning to me. "What the fuck are you crying for?"

"IpunchedAngelaandhernosestartedblee-hee-heeeeeeediiiiiiiing," I said, without taking a breath.

"Oh, Jesus H. Christ," Grandma said, getting up. "Why did you punch her?"

"She was changing the ruuuuuules."

"So?"

I couldn't tell if she was being nonchalant about the fact that Angela was being a bitch or that I thought violence was the correct way to deal with it, but I stopped crying while I tried to figure it out.

"Listen—did she hit you back?"

"No. I ran away."

Grandma tilted her head and raised her eyebrows in complete disbelief. "You ran away from a fight?"

"She was bleeding," I said, leaving a glistening trail of snot across my forearm as I dragged it under my nose.

"Get a goddamn tissue." Grandma went to the back door. A minute later, she stomped back in a way that indicated I was in deep shit. I must have hurt Angela more than I thought. I started crying again. She crossed to the foyer and leaned right in my face, pointing her finger under my dripping nose.

"Shut up, child. She's fine—they're out there right now, playing the game without you. Is that what you want? To be left out? To run away like a baby?" She had the habit of stringing so many questions together that I didn't know how to answer. I shook my head. Then nodded my head. Then shook my head.

"You never run away from a fight, y'hear me? You start it, you finish it." Her eyes were wide and wild. Her dentures slipped forward slightly with every hard *T* sound she hit. "If you don't go back out there and beat that little girl's ass, you're gonna have to come in here and fight *me*."

"I don't want to finish it."

"That's too fucking bad."

Tears started dripping from my head again, prompted by the bone-deep confusion running through me. I came into the house looking for comfort, having just punched my former best friend directly in the face, but was somehow instead being forced to choose between fighting Angela *again* or punching my own grandmother.

"You gonna go back out there?"

"Nooooo," I wailed, fully focused now on whether I'd be able to even land a punch on Grandma, let alone win a fight with her. Not only was she stocky and low to the ground, but she apparently had no qualms about getting into a fistfight with a minor. What if I made her nose bleed, too?

"Go upstairs. Whew, you look ugly when you cry," she said. This was her go-to whenever we cried in her presence; I used to think she was trying to make us smile, but now that I'm older I think she was just a little bit sadistic and only doing it to make herself laugh. "And get a tissue. Such a baby. It was one punch," she added, grabbing the Nintendo controller and sitting back down on the kitchen chair.

I ran upstairs and threw myself on my bed. Moments later, Cory came running in, the front door slamming behind him.

"You kids better stop running in and out of this house!" I could hear Grandma yell beneath me. Our bedroom was right over the living room, but she was so loud I would have heard her from school.

"I need a paper towel!" Cory was breathless. "Angela's nose is bleeding."

"I already heard about it. What do you want me to do, sound

the fire alarm? My god, you kids act like you've never been in a fight before. All I did was fight when I was your age!"

Cory's quick footsteps pounded back toward the door before it slammed shut again.

"If I lose one more goddamn life in this game because of you kids I will come out there and punch *all* of you in the nose, then we'll see who's *really* crying!" Grandma screamed after him.

I was bereft. I felt out of control—my anger surprised me, but the fear of losing Angela's friendship scared the shit out of me. I didn't understand how I could feel those two things so distinctly— I hated her, was furious with her, but also didn't want her to know how angry she made me. I was scared to take the risk of being alone, the risk that what I thought was actually true: at some point, everyone is going to abandon me.

Grandma was doing her best to make me tough. Whenever I asked, she would tell me stories about being a kid in Harlem—jumping from one rooftop to another, playing jacks in alleys, her friend getting bitten by a dog—and about all of the people she fought or stood up to. For Grandma, being tough and independent was the only way to survive, so I had to learn how to survive in a new way. I learned a lot from her about how to stand up for myself, to use my voice, how to make up my own mind. She also taught me how to lose.

In the Henderson household, board games were a competitive sport, with Grandma acting as the Commodus to my Maximus.

The suggestion to even play had to come from her; I would occasionally run into the living room, breathless, holding the Parcheesi box while she sat on the couch chain-smoking, and ask if she wanted to play. "Not now. I'm busy," she would say, taking another drag and staring off into space. I started to notice that if I sat in the living room reading long enough on a Saturday afternoon, she'd throw me a bone: "Want to play Monopoly?" Perhaps the bent, jagged form of an overgrown eleven-year-old with a dowager's hump reminded her that children need brain-building activities and mental stimulation. Mostly she just loved any chance to show off.

"Go get your brother." Everyone knows that playing a board game with two people is a useless endeavor, but it was also rare that the three of us were in the house at the same time. If I wanted to play, the last hurdle was finding and convincing Cory to join in.

A game of Monopoly paled in comparison to the Evel Knievel lifestyle Cory was fashioning for himself, so I usually had to throw in a bribe.

"I'll buy you a slice of pizza!"

He stopped wailing a branch against the side of the house to throw me a squinty-eyed look.

"You don't have any money," he said, suspicious.

"Sweetie Pie sent me a check for five dollars for my birthday."

". . . Okay."

We always gathered in exactly the same seats around the kitchen table and used exactly the same pieces every time—Grandma was the top hat, Cory was the race car, and I was the dog. Grandma was always the banker. "You're not good at math," she said, pointing her cigarette at me. "And you're a thief," she said to a wide-eyed Cory. "You think I don't see you trying to slip hundreds out of the tray?"

Copying Grandma, we slipped the tips of our Crayola-colored money about a quarter of an inch under the board, copying the order of the money in the bank. I get the impression from friends that their family game nights were always a fun and low-key affair—you drank soda, laughed, and delighted in winning a few rounds. The board game boxes themselves advertised smiling white people huddled around game pieces, unable to believe all the fun they are having. A complete lie. My grandma spent her childhood fighting rats in order to carve out enough space to play jacks against the wall in a New York City alley, trying to win money for penny candy. She was a proto Peaky Blinder, and in her world, every game was a blood sport meant to be won at all costs. After rolling to see who went first, the Monopoly carnage began in earnest.

Grandma sat at the head of the table, looking down her glasses coolly, pausing for an eternity before deciding whether to buy every property she landed on.

"Come on, Grandma!" I was instantly impatient. I'd been down this road with her before. "You know you're going to buy it!"

"I might not," she said, resting her hands under her chin like a cartoon villain, staring at the board.

Cory and I would start to flail and sigh in our chairs, not realizing that this interminable wait was part of her strategy to bring us to our knees. After what felt like several hours, she would look up and say, "I'll take it." She bought everything. Every railroad. Park Place. Marvin Gardens. She had monopolies before we even passed Go the first time, and hotels erected on her properties just as we were starting to buy whatever was left over. After tucking her property card neatly behind the others, she would smile benevolently at her bounty.

The same patience was not afforded to me when it was my turn. "Just buy the property, child," Grandma said, unable to appreciate the ways I was trying to mimic her because she'd moved on to another tool in her arsenal—straight-up bullying.

"I don't know if I want Baltic." I had no real reason for denying any property other than the low rent.

"Buy it, you're holding up the whole game."

Cory was always inexplicably excited to buy the cheap properties. "Wait until I put hotels up," he said, barely able to contain his anticipation of impending slumlordship.

I always caved, eager to own something, anything, that would keep me in the game; after Grandma bought anything worth having, the only chance for survival was to have something she needed.

"I'll trade you Connecticut if you give me Indiana," she said calmly, looking down her glasses, the card dangling between her fingertips like a piece of garbage she collected from the street.

"But that would give you a Monopoly on the reds."

"I'll throw in five hundred dollars."

Sometimes Cory and I would try to protect each other from her negotiating tactics. "Don't sell to her, Dani! She's gonna make so much money now!" Grandma didn't even turn her head toward the direction of the interference. "Am I negotiating with him, or with you?" She raised her eyebrows, her stare simultaneously nonchalant and aggressive. I looked at that brightly colored bill and thought how much it would buy.

"Okay!"

"Thank you kindly," Grandma said, properties and money ex-changing hands.

Once we started negotiating, it wasn't long before I was wiped out. Every game ended the same way: Grandma lorded over her winnings like a queen surveying her kingdom while I tried to pinpoint which horrible decision brought about my downfall.

It was the loser's job to clean up. I was organizing bills by color and stuffing them back into the slick plastic tray, putting metal pieces under the cardboard instruction flap, when, deep in my anger, I shouted, "Angela's mom always lets us win when we play games with her!"

Grandma flipped her head back so hard I thought she might snap her neck and let out a laugh like a machine-gun blast. "*Let* you win? *Let* you? Honey, that's for white people. In this house, you earn it."

13.

Grandma handed me a ten-dollar bill from the pocket of her black polyester pants, the elastic waistband resting comfortably on her round belly. Shirtless and wearing only a white bra, she leaned toward the mirror over the bathroom sink, angling her tweezers toward an errant chin hair. I casually noticed that one of her tits was as big as my head and was still spilling over the top of her bra. Every part of her body seemed to point extremely forward.

"The green box."

"For your period?"

"No."

"Then why am I buying you maxi pads?"

She used her other hand to pull her cheek skin taut and squinted her eyes. "Sometimes you just . . . y'know. Leak a little."

"Leak *what*?"

"Will you go to the goddamn store, please?"

Thrusting the ten dollars into my own pocket, I stomped away, slamming the front door. No one ever answered my questions all the way; Grandma told me to look it up in the encyclopedia, and Mrs. Bell made me go to the library during study hall to cruise the card catalog and look up any answers that weren't contained in our social studies or math books. The World Book encyclopedia people skipped the "Leaking Grandma" section somehow.

I was twelve years old, and I missed my mom. Our bathroom conversations were more fun, back in Greenwood Lake when she would pop out her teeth and blow my mind. Grandma popped out her teeth in an old-lady way, expected and unimpressive. Would Mom make me buy her maxi pads? The last time we had lived together, I hadn't been old enough to go to the grocery store alone.

She still called sometimes. If Grandma answered, I could tell it was Mom on the other end by the way Grandma sucked in her breath and said, "What do you want?" before shoving the phone at me. "Your mother," she'd say, glancing at the TV during the hand-off. She only talked about Mom's absence when she was annoyed at something she had to do for us, like school shopping. "Your mother should be doing this," she'd grumble while I shoved my feet in the shoe-measuring contraption at Buster Brown. I didn't talk about Mom with Cory, whose life still seemed to carry on effortlessly in her absence. Mom disappeared from our day-to-day lives, the phone our only reminder, our only connection.

Mom's voice disarmed me. She sounded the same, like nothing had happened. I wanted to be tough, to give only monosyllabic answers and feign indifference while she told me about her new job at the discount store on Gun Hill Road, the offices she sometimes cleaned at night, the job Luke found that he would no longer have by the next time she called. She spoke with the same lilt in her voice, the same nasal way she called me *Dani*. The same Mom.

I cried despite myself.

"Take it in the kitchen," Grandma said, unable to hear her show over my anguish. I looped my fingers around the empty space in the back of the phone and dragged the long cord into the kitchen. I tried to keep it down as I asked Mom when she was coming to get us between sobs.

It was always the same answer: soon. Or maybe, she ventured, she would come get me and Cory to live with her in the city.

I cried harder. Mom tried to tell me the city wasn't bad, I'd get used to it, I'd make friends. She didn't realize I was crying at the thought of living with Luke again. I didn't tell her the extent of what he did to me; she was living in this fantasy of a family, ignoring the rot at the center, making us lie and cover for all the abuse Luke inflicted on us. I couldn't even process that she was excited about reuniting with me and Cory—she still lived with Luke, and I didn't trust her anymore.

She tried to soothe me by telling me how fantastic her life was. She was doing well. Everything was great. She loved me and missed me and couldn't wait to see me. I was spinning in space, living life backward and upside down, getting used to the fact that she could be perfectly settled while we were apart. When I first moved in with Grandma and Granddad, I desperately wanted to go back to a time when it was just the three of us, for Mom to finally, for once, choose me. But she was fine without me. I ended our phone calls with less hope each time.

I kicked a rock on my way up the hill to Main Street and left it at the corner when I crossed to go to the Grand Union. I hadn't yet gotten my period, and I certainly didn't want to get it—I cared less about preparing my body for the children I already knew I did not want to have and more about the pain-in-the-ass monthly maintenance of the whole bloody display. I made a silent vow as I dodged a car backing out of a parking space: if I still had my period by the time I was as old as Grandma, I would have a plug surgically implanted or have all my reproductive organs ripped out. And if I started leaking, I would lower myself into a shallow grave, pull loose dirt over my body, and smother myself to death.

The automatic door whooshed open. I knew exactly where to go, but first I had to do my rounds. I cruised by the vegetables to the deli counter at the back of the store, then started weaving in and out of the aisles to make sure I didn't see anyone I knew. Buying maxi pads was embarrassing enough; buying maxi pads in plain view of Mitra McLaughlin's mother was a devastating blow to the psyche. The last time Grandma asked me to buy her pads I quickly rounded the corner on my way to the cashier and ran into Irene, one of her old card-playing friends from Greenwood Lake.

"Hi, Dani!" She glanced at the box of embarrassment tucked under my arm like a football. "You're getting to be such a big girl."

It was bad enough that I was still very much a little girl, with a body so tall and flat I had corners, but it was even harder to explain that I was buying these pads for her possibly incontinent friend. I'd just smiled and walked away instead, my cheeks burning as I shook my head to cast off the shame of discovery.

The coast was clear. I made my way to the last hurdle. I skipped the teenage cashiers—older siblings of the assholes I had to sit next to every day—and waited until I could scope out the oldest woman standing behind a register. "Brown bag, please," I corrected as I watched her put the pads in a plastic bag that was too transparent for such a delicate purchase. She looked at me from under her nest of hairsprayed, frosted blond bangs, and handed me the plastic bag.

I walked quickly across the parking lot. The green box of Always pads was like the light on the dock in *The Great Gatsby*, signaling to all who were near that right in their midst was a twelve-year-old girl dying of embarrassment.

I bolted into the house, where Grandma was pacing in the living room. "What the fuck took you so long! I'm going to be late for work!" She'd finally had to find a job, as it became clear we weren't going anywhere, and she ended up at Mount Alverno, a sort of retirement home for nuns, run by the Franciscan Sisters of the Poor. Grandma worked in the Greenbrier Room, a big dining hall that served catered meals every day to anyone who could afford it.

She grabbed the bag out of my hands and walked toward the bathroom. "The store is three minutes away—it shouldn't take you damn near an hour to get these," she called over her shoulder.

She not only sent me on the most embarrassing errand possible, but she had the nerve to put a clock on it. My mouth was in action before my synapses could spark the part of my brain that knew better.

"You should have told me to rush, then!" I regretted the words as soon as I said them. This was primetime back talk, highest rank-ing on the endless list of things Grandma would not tolerate. I walked quickly to the living room and plopped on the couch so she wouldn't have time to physically snatch me, but she was in my face by the time I sat down on the couch.

"What did you say to me, fuck-o?" Her eyes were as wide as her skin would stretch them.

"Nothing," I said meekly.

"That's what I thought." She walked back to the bathroom, a tiny tugboat of righteous anger.

When she made her way back to the living room to grab her purse, I tried a different approach.

"I don't want to buy those anymore." It was a moment of ex-treme stupidity, brought on by my desire to have something in my life that didn't make me feel so out of place.

Grandma threw her purse over her shoulder and adjusted her black bowtie. Her work uniform was formal, but she had a way of making it look like something a fancy boxer would wear. Grandma in the ring, shirtless and wearing only an industrial bra, elastic-waist polyester pants, slowly pulling off her bowtie as someone slipped in her mouth guard.

"Too fucking bad," she said, slamming the front door behind her.

Unlike most girls my age, I tried not to consider my body. I didn't compare it to models' in magazines. I didn't pray for my period. I didn't weigh myself or examine my face carefully in the mirror. I went through most days without thinking about my body at all. So I had no frame of reference when, one morning, I woke up completely frozen.

I was awake, but I couldn't move a muscle.

I could hear the cable trucks kicking up pebbles against our garbage cans as they pulled into the lot, Jane Pauley starting another hour of the *Today* show on the TV I had left on all night. Grandma would be upset that I was running up the electric bill, but the voices from the TV made me feel less afraid as I was preparing myself for sleep that would rarely come. I was thankful for cable; the network channels got boring at night, right before they played the national anthem over an image of an American flag and turned off for the night.

I was completely unable to move. I tried talking myself into action. *Open your mouth. Open your mouth.* If I could scream, someone would come upstairs to see what was wrong. Or, more likely, someone would come upstairs to yell at me for screaming. Still, someone would come if I could move, if I could only move. *Open your mouth.* Nothing, not even a twitch. The *Today* show would be back after these messages.

Was I in a coma? Grandma wouldn't have the patience to sit next to me in a hospital and read books to me like they did in the movies. I would be at the mercy of the nurses and candy stripers. Would my teachers send work to the hospital so that I could stay with my class when I woke up? Or would I be a twenty-year-old with a fifth-grade education, stuck in time? I might not ever wake up; then it wouldn't matter.

If I could just move my mouth.

I wasn't moving, no matter how hard I tried. I suddenly had the thought that I should try to go back to sleep—like a hard reset, a do-over. I let the commercials calm me, listening to the TV and the sounds of outside until I went back to sleep.

It worked. According to the *Today* show schedule, it took almost an hour for me to wake up fully. I felt slightly numb and was vibrating with tension. I waved my hand in front of my face, wiggled my toes, wiggled my jaw back and forth, making sure everything worked the way it did before I was paralyzed.

The sleep paralysis started happening a few times a week. I never got used to it, but I did start panicking less when I realized that it would eventually just fix itself. It could have been my insomnia, or it could have been the aftermath of what I survived. Sleep paralysis was just another thing that kept me connected to Luke, another way my body still felt tied to trauma.

I felt it in other ways, too, like when I found that I couldn't look at my body in the gym mirror, or the time my English teacher tried to teach us to meditate. The strangeness I felt when I closed my eyes in a classroom full of my peers was compounded by the feeling of waking up around them. I looked at Meg and Amy, both of them repressing giggles. Whatever had just happened, I felt lighter than I did when I walked in the room. But I'd also felt like I'd lost time. Was that the point of this? To lull us into complacency? Anything could have happened while she had us in such a relaxed state. What Luke did to me felt like this—powerlessness, surrender. As quickly as the feeling of lightness washed over me, more intense feelings of shame and anger replaced it. I'm still not at ease in my body. This, too, had been taken from me.

14.

When I was younger, the arrival of summer meant that you were forced to be outside for days on end. As I became a teenager, pop culture had led me to believe that summers were for lazing around, swimming, and snacking. But this white, middle-class worldview was not shared by Grandma. When she was my age, people were still shoving kids down mines without ventilators to stand on tightropes or construct bombs that only their tiny hands could manage, so she couldn't really stomach the small generational shift that resulted in her granddaughter wanting to read all day. Most days I slept as late as possible, waking up only when the sun rose so high in the sky that the heat streaming through the open windows became unbearable. If I wasn't up by the time Grandma left for work, she'd shout upstairs and wake me up with her choice of monologues about my useless childhood.

"Dani! Dan-ee-yell! It's ten a.m.! Get up! You kids think you can sleep all day like there's nothing to do around here. I've *never* seen such laziness in my *life*," she lied. The fact that my uncle— who hadn't worked in two years—was currently smoking himself to death in the room across the landing shone a bright light on the charade. I would rouse myself enough to stand at the top of the steps and shout, "I'm *up*," then take myself right back to bed.

As soon as he heard the front door close, Uncle Bobby always moved from his room to the living room for a change of scenery. It had a bigger TV and the family VCR, so he settled in and commandeered it before I had a chance to camp out for the day. He always had a snide comment for me whenever I dragged myself downstairs.

"It's one o'clock—don't you have anything to do today?"

"I'm on summer vacation—this *is* what I'm supposed to do today. Don't *you* have a job or something?"

"Go outside."

"Get a job," I called over my shoulder on the way to the bathroom. My uncle and I had a fairly compact "Take My Wife" routine for two people who were not married and couldn't stand the sight of each other.

Since my friends all lived on the outskirts of town and all three of the adults in my house didn't drive, I spent most of my summer in town. I would fill my days with walks to the library, reading in silence in my room, and playing Little League softball. Sometimes we would go to the lake with our neighbors. Ben was a kind, intelligent blond kid who loved music; he was in my class, but he mostly hung out with Cory. His single mother, Diane, was a tiny superstar; I liked seeing her Dorothy Hamill bob power-walking down Main Street, almost a foot below everyone else on the sidewalk. She's actually average in height, but I was already in the process of reaching my full monstrous height, so everyone seemed much smaller. In a couple of years, she would start her own photography studio, sometimes using me as a model for practice, but she had been taking beautiful photos long before she branched out on her own. Diane would pile me, Cory, and Ben into her car and drive us to the lake at Wawayanda. The air felt ten degrees cooler as she curled and twisted the car deep into the woods.

The lake was ringed by tall, lush trees; I liked to dig my toes into the sand, pick a tree in the distance, and try to swim out to it. I never made it all the way across, but the sweeter reward was waiting for me back on the beach, where I'd throw myself on a towel and let the sun warm me as the water evaporated from my skin. No one gave a shit about sunscreen; we rubbed ourselves down with baby oil like fucking idiots and crisped ourselves on bath towels like strips of bacon. For most people, summer wasn't in full swing until the straps of your bathing suit left grill marks on your shoulders, or you could peel long strips of blistered skin from your back like a sheet of loose-leaf paper. For me, a fair-skinned person with freckles, a hearty sunburn was my way of saying to people, *Look, I've been outside this summer, at least once. Please don't ask me to do this again.*

My softball games were always at night; this gave parents a

chance to see how their recessive traits showed up in their children as we clumsily tried to field pop flies. Grandma showed up once or twice, but I was on my own for daytime practices and most games.

Buying baseball cards was an important part of my week; walking to Main Street and stopping at Dayton's was sometimes all the sun I would get during the day. Baseball was the only thing that could take me away from books, and spending entire days inside.

Dayton's was a dusty jumble of a store. It was the kind of place where you could get a box fan, an off-brand radio, hair products recently out of production, scratchy comforters, and plungers. I stuck to the candy and magazine section. It was the first aisle you hit when you walked in the store, making it easy for the cashier at the raised platform register on the left to see Cory and his friends as they tried to steal Snickers bars.

I always waved to Wayne, the stocky owner with the Friar Tuck ring of graying hair clinging to the sides of his head. He had the worn-down tiredness of a middle-aged dad, but I don't know if he had any kids. He never seemed to follow or watch me, probably because I had the permanently shame-filled face of someone who would rather throw herself in traffic before stealing anything ever again. I said hello as a matter of course in local friendliness but also to let him know that I knew he was there and wasn't about to try anything out of sorts. I looked for the new issues of *Bop* and *Teen Beat*, *Rolling Stone* or any magazine featuring a guitar on the front, and sometimes bought a comic book if there was a lady on the front and she looked cool.

"How old are you now?" Wayne was walking by with a box that was big enough to hold a TV.

"Twelve. Thirteen next month."

He nodded and kept walking, stepping out of the path of a customer on his way to the back of the store.

This time I spied something on the rack that I'd never seen before, or never noticed. *Sassy* magazine was instantly more macabre than the bright pink, bubble-letter covers of the teenybopper magazines I usually purchased. The logo looked like someone slashed paint against a wall. The articles had weird, intriguing titles, like "Our Writer Knee-Deep in Mud at an English Rave" or "What Jail Is Like for Girls." The cover model was traditionally beautiful, but with an underlying spookiness in her heavily lined eyes.

I added it to my stack, bought two ten-cent boxes of Lemonheads, and walked home. I didn't even crack open *Bop*—I flipped through *Sassy* first, and by the time I finished reading the issue, I was mailing in the card for a subscription.

I felt like I was looking at a portal to another world. It was the first magazine I read that was for teenage girls but the content wasn't exclusively about boys—it was written by and for young women. The models and writers were often one in the same, wearing dresses made out of pillowcases and documenting how they shaved their heads. It read like a letter from a big sister, or what I imagined a big sister would say to me as she made her way out of Warwick and into the world. There were pop culture references I didn't immediately get, but the books and music they recommended sent me down a rabbit hole of discovery. Instead of the pandering, sugarcoated nonsense that passed as news in most teen mags, whenever I read *Sassy* I felt like I actually learned something about a part of the human experience, like what it was like to grow up on a reservation or live with an eating disorder. In a world full of things telling me that the existence of teenage girls was a frivolous annoyance, this was a magazine that took girls seriously.

And, most importantly, some of their models were Black. Girls like me, looking cool and comfortable.

It sparked something in me to see girls my own age doing things their own way. My world was so small—everyone looked the same, wanted the same things, talked the same way. Being Black kept me outside of the bubble; even though I had friends, they always pointed out things that were different about me as a source of some inherent freakiness, like the fact that I didn't wash my hair every day or live with my mom.

Maybe I didn't have to try so hard. Maybe it was okay, and even cool, that I couldn't afford to buy brand-new clothes, instead relying on the thrift store and creativity. Maybe it was okay that I didn't want to spend all day talking about boys and crushes, or try to look like all the perfect, pretty, rich white girls who surrounded me. The more I read about girls who lived in cities, on the street, or in the middle of nowhere, the less shame I felt about being different.

From the itchy Sears-covered comfort of my own bed, I read about ways to bring the inside out, ways to set myself free. If *Sassy* laid the fire, cable TV lit the match.

The only time I got to watch the big TV during the summer was when Uncle Bobby went out to buy cigarettes. Even though I had a small TV in my bedroom, the living room TV had the VCR. As soon as I heard the front door click shut, I raced downstairs and turned on HBO or MTV.

One day, I caught the end of a movie that looked promising

because the high school exploded; I flipped through the *TV Guide* to find out what it was called and when it would be on next, and asked Grandma if I could borrow one of her soap opera tapes to record it. Then all I had to do was wait for a day when Uncle Bobby would leave the fucking house so I could watch it from the beginning.

I can't tell you whether *Heathers* is objectively good. I can only say that within the span of four weeks I watched that movie so many times that I have every line of it memorized to this day. My town was filled with Heathers, and this was the first time I saw anything shine a light on the cruelty of popularity instead of venerating it. I already felt confident in my hatred of the cliquey, mean girls who ruled the middle school, but seeing that hatred reflected back to me was more validating than watching Darryl Strawberry hit a home run or finally learning how to slide.

Warwick took on a sheen of impermanence. I could go anywhere, be anyone. I didn't want to be like my mom, to give my life over to men. I couldn't conceive of a life that revolved around or even involved men. And I didn't want to be like my classmates, either, to plan a life around college, marriage, and babies. I never hung a pillowcase over my hair and pretended it was a veil. Playing house was boring.

I could fill my life with art. I could travel. I could skip college or go to one that had more people like me there. That summer, I discovered that there was more than one path. Nothing that was happening around me had to dictate who I was or who I could become.

I could survive this town.

15.

Your mother is coming up tomorrow." Grandma informed me of this earth-shattering news with the nonchalance of someone asking me for the time. We were sitting on the couch, watching the news. My guts started to bubble.

"So what? I don't want to see her."

I hadn't physically been in the same room with Mom for almost two years. Or him.

"Is he coming with her?" I asked quietly, biting my thumbnail.

"The asshole? Probably. Get your hand out of your mouth." Grandma couldn't stand my nail-biting. "Such a nasty habit."

She used to bite her nails and told me the same story every time she caught me biting mine: "You know how I stopped? I went on a date with your grandfather, and he held my hand. When he looked at my nails he said, 'Ew!' and I dropped my hand. I never bit my nails again."

Nothing about this was in character for Grandma. "Why didn't you punch him or dump him?" I wanted to know.

"I liked him."

I thought about Luke and put my thumbnail back between my teeth. I would chew my fingers down to the knuckle if it kept men away from me.

I'd never seen this car before, some old mustard yellow thing. I was kneeling in front of one of the living room windows, peeking out from behind the curtain. Luke was hunched over the steering wheel. Mom got out of the passenger side, slammed the door, and opened the back door. Her hair was different, pulled back into a tight bun on top of her head.

Cory heard the door slam and came bounding down the stairs. "They're here!" he said, running outside. He threw himself around Mom's waist and curled his hands below her belly button, taking her by surprise. He was crying. She turned around and hugged him. How could he still love her this much? Luke got out of the car and unbuckled Luke Jr. from the seat behind him. The Baby was as tall as the side mirrors of the car now.

Grandma was sitting on the couch, looking out the window. "Can you believe this shit?" she said, rising to get a closer look.

"She has another goddamn baby in that car." Sure enough, after Mom released Cory's grip, she reached into the car and pulled out a carrier. A small, puffy face peered out from under the soft blanket wrapped around it. Mom was all smiles.

I burst into tears. "I don't want to meet it!" Beyond my immediate fury was a chasm of pain. She left us here and had more kids. She loved him enough to have another kid. He was never going away.

Grandma stubbed out her cigarette. "Oh, stop being such a pain in the ass. It's a baby," she said with a scowl, adding under her breath, "That girl doesn't know her ass from her elbow; she has no business having another baby."

Mom was still hugging Cory with one hand, maneuvering the carrier with the other. "Dani," she called blindly into the house, "come out and meet your little brother!" As she started walking toward the front porch, I ran to the couch and crossed my arms over my chest. My head was down when she walked in the front door, but I heard the carrier bang against the doorframe as she came in.

"Hi, Robin," Grandma said plainly.

"Hi, Ma," she said. She sounded exhausted. "This is Christian!"

Grandma started smiling and cooing at the baby swaddled in the car seat. Babies were her soft spot; every time I told her I didn't ever want to give birth to one, she drifted off to a more gentle place and talked about how much she loved raising her babies. It was a weakness in her that I resented. *Get your shit together*, I thought. *We're supposed to hate Mom the same.*

I was still rooted to the couch, so Mom came over and hugged me. The familiarity of her arms around me made me feel like I had just been punched in the chest. I couldn't breathe; my cry was caught in my throat.

"What's the matter, Dani?" Mom said, rubbing my back. "It's okay, sweetheart, it's okay."

I inhaled, still pressed against her chest. "I missed you!" Each word came out staccato, followed by a forceful, chest-crushing sob. I pulled myself away from her and threw my hands to my face. Still sitting, I curled down, trying to press myself through the couch, into the ground, wanting to disappear. I was mad at myself for crying, for admitting to myself how much I still needed her.

"It's okay, sweetheart," Mom said sweetly. "Here, have a tissue. Luke, hand me the tissues."

With all the crying, I didn't register that Luke was in the room. Suddenly, his hand was under my chin, holding a green box of Grand Union–brand tissues.

"Hi, Dani."

Grandma was in the armchair, leaning forward to make noises at the new baby, still in the carrier on the floor in front of her. Cory was jumping up and down in place, unable to contain his excitement. I'd never told anyone what happened. If Grandma knew, would she even let him in the house? Look at her, forgetting her hatred so quickly. I was alone.

I couldn't look at him. What was I before him? I barely remembered. Me before him, sleeping through the night, my body and brain waking up at the same time instead of being pinned to the bed, paralyzed. I hadn't known that someone could touch me in any way that wasn't full of love. I hadn't wanted to sink into the earth or disappear like a dried-out dandelion being blown apart.

I took a tissue to catch the snot dripping toward my lap like a slow faucet.

"Say thank you," Mom said.

"Thank you," I said to my lap, unable to stop the knee-jerk reaction to Mom's invective. She taught me this. How to be kind, passive. He used that kindness to hurt me, to shame me into silence.

He was here, always here. Taking her further and further away from me, even when we were in the same room. Somewhere along the way, I had done something wrong. But what was it? What makes a mother leave? What makes a mother leave and have more kids?

She knew, I thought. The bruises I was afraid to explain. Walking into her bedroom and finding me next to him while he snored, facedown and naked next to me. Her ultimate punishment was leaving me behind, to get me away from him so she could have him all to herself. New kids to replace her old, rotten one. She didn't love me. How could she? I was ugly, too big, too loud. Every day she wasn't here with us, she was choosing him.

Hating him didn't matter. I hated myself more.

16.

My great-granddad's real name was John Lacey, but everyone called him Showboat. Usually when members of my family came in from the city to visit, it was a loud, raucous, all-day event filled with food, card games, and shit-talking people who had the nerve to not be there. Showboat always showed up alone—and only once a year—to help Grandma with her taxes. He had deep, watery brown eyes and a light, raspy voice. His gray mustache always threatened to poke me in the eye when he kissed me on the cheek. He came from an era when men didn't leave the house without putting on a suit, so his presence instantly felt old-fashioned to me. He moved slowly and with intent. He reminded me of the dude who sat on a mushroom and smoked in the *Alice in Wonderland* cartoon. There was something gentle about him that made me feel at ease. He never removed his jacket during the entire visit, no matter how long it took for them to finish. He was never that comfortable.

Showboat and Grandma didn't act like fathers and daughters I'd seen in TV or the movies. There were none of the grand gestures of reuniting—no tears, no stories, no remember-whens.

"Hi, Pudge," he said as Grandma closed the door, moving from the foyer into the living room. Grandma gave him a quick hug and kissed him on the cheek. She didn't smile, laugh, or react to the fact that he called her Pudge. She hadn't spent all night frying chicken, and he didn't walk in with a bowl of black-eyed peas. As far as family visits went, this was already a much more somber affair.

"You have a job yet?" Showboat asked me as he eased himself onto a chair at the kitchen table. He was wearing a gray suit and had already put his brown hat on the coatrack in the closet.

"No!" I laughed. "I'm only twelve."

"Plenty old enough for a job in my day," he said with a wink. "Your job is to keep doing good in school."

"Who's Pudge?" I asked, indignant.

Cory was nowhere to be found; he might bounce in later, but we weren't lined up for inspection and forced to be in the house as everyone arrived. I stayed around because I was curious; before this visit, I'd only met Showboat once, and at the time, I hadn't even known he was Grandma's dad.

"Pudge," he said, turning his glossy eyes to me, "is your grandmother. Been calling her that since she was a little thing."

"Why?"

"Because I was fat," Grandma said, stubbing out the cigarette she'd left burning in the ashtray on the coffee table. She pointed at Showboat. "Coffee?"

"Thank you." He looked after her as she walked into the kitchen, then turned to me and winked again. "She really was pudgy." He puffed out his cheeks, his eyes wide. I was delighted to learn new information about someone I thought I'd already known everything about.

"What were your friends like at my age?" I snuck in questions about Grandma's childhood whenever I could. Her stories were always wild and funny and brought New York City to life.

"We just did our own thing," she said, her eyes never leaving the screen. "Jumped rooftops, played caps in the alley, that sort of thing."

Everything about Child Grandma astounded me. She had always been exactly this tough, talking casually about the constant threat of danger that passed for fun when she was my age. It was like learning about the Civil War from a soldier who had lost a leg on the battlefield.

Showboat and Sweetie Pie were divorced, and had been since Grandma and her sister, my great-aunt Connie, were little. Showboat was a retired IRS accountant; when Grandma got her first ever tax-paying job at the convent, she called him for help. Granddad was never around for the visit; he was paid cash under the table at the bar where he worked, so a former IRS accountant digging through his annual earnings was about as useful to him as a mop made entirely of dicks. Calling Showboat made sense, but it was simultaneously a display of Grandma's frugality and vindictiveness to ask her estranged father to sit in a room with her all day rather than pay someone local a few bucks.

"Go play outside—we're busy," Grandma said, coming into the kitchen with her ashtray, shooing me away with her free hand. I was hunched over the table on my elbows, my knees digging into the cushioned seat of a kitchen chair. Papers were spread out on the table.

"It's cold out!" I knew this wouldn't be a realistic excuse for staying inside, but I was curious.

"Then go upstairs and read a book. Just be quiet, for god's sake. This is grown-up time."

Showboat winked at me again and clicked open his briefcase as I hopped off the chair and walked away, dejected. "Okay, Pudge, what have you got for me?"

<hr />

The next year when Showboat came up, I was determined to find out what the hell they were doing. By the time they came into the kitchen, I was already sitting at the table.

"We're just doing my taxes, Dani," Grandma sighed. They were in the same spots at the kitchen table where they sat the year before.

"Why?"

"You have to, it's the law."

"Why?"

"Income tax helps pay for things that towns and cities need to help people," Showboat said. I bristled at the *Sesame Street* explanation. I wanted to know all the important things about being a grown-up, not the kid version.

"I know."

"Oh, you do?" Showboat's eyebrows were raised.

I quickly skirted past my lie. "Yeah, but how do you do it? The taxes."

"Well, first you have to have a job."

"I could babysit now, but I can't get my working papers until I'm fourteen." It was shockingly true that most girls my age started babysitting when we were twelve or thirteen. Parents weighed the hefty responsibility of children against the expectations of a pre-teen who didn't know about minimum-wage laws, and took the cheap route every time.

"Okay, let's do your taxes based on babysitting, then. Here, pull your chair over." He motioned to the spot next to him and scooted over a little to make room.

"We don't have time for this," Grandma said. I knew this voice, the tight one she used just before she got really angry. Bruce Banner about to turn into the Incredible Hulk.

"It'll be quick. We're just having fun." Showboat moved some papers around the table. Grandma stubbed out her cigarette and walked out of the room.

"Call me when you're done."

Showboat pointed his gold pen at a box on the form. "This says annual earnings. What do you think that means?"

I thought about it. "Money for one year?"

"Very good! So how much money did you make this year? Just any old number."

"Five thousand dollars."

"You didn't work very hard, then," he joked. He wrote "$5,000" in the box.

We worked through the form together, using fractions and subtraction to calculate my made-up tax on my made-up income. "How much money does Grandma make?" I asked cautiously. We never openly discussed how much money my grandparents earned— we just fought about how much they didn't have when it came to buying stuff I wanted.

"More than five thousand dollars."

"One hundred thousand dollars?"

Showboat laughed. "Less than one hundred thousand dollars." He looked at me. "You have everything you need, right?"

I thought about it, then nodded.

"Then don't worry about how much money Pudge makes. You have enough to worry about," he said, tapping his pen on the forms, "since your employer didn't pay any taxes at all for you, and *you* just found out taxes exist."

Grandma came back in, raring to go. "Okay, enough, we have things to do before he misses his bus."

I left the kitchen on the wave of another wink as Showboat and Grandma got to work.

When I finally got the small blue card from the state of New York that said I was eligible for restricted work, a year later, I applied at the local toy store.

I'd never shopped in there; the store opened when I was too old for toys, and they sold expensive brands I didn't recognize, like Breyer and Playmobil. Most of the toys were made of plain wood or were bright puzzles that were actually homework in disguise. I was hired to work weekends and a few days a week in the summer, switching to only weekends during the school year. My main duties were dusting, straightening up after the spoiled monsters who tore through the store while their uninterested moms talked near the front door, and vacuuming after we closed. I earned $4.25 per hour and worked around ten hours a week. I also started babysitting for Helen Truitt, my coworker.

I worked with Helen most of the time and instantly adored her. She had a calm demeanor, kind blue eyes, and a sick sense of humor that was complementary to my own. One day, I was dusting the counter displays near the register and picked up a giant, hollow plastic dinosaur. I picked a bunch of stones out of the small display of rocks and gems and jammed them in the dinosaur's open mouth. Helen was sitting behind the register.

"Hey. Hey, lady," I said in a joke voice, making the dinosaur hop around a little on the glass countertop. "I'm Chunky, the puking dinosaur." I tipped the toy toward the counter, and all the rocks and gems spilled out while I made fake throw-up noises.

Helen's laugh started as a low stutter and turned into a full-on shriek. Making her laugh became my favorite reason to go to work.

Chunky the Puking Dinosaur became a constant inside joke, but we lived to make each other laugh through the commonality of our grade-school sense of humor—making sure the Playmobil display figures were always bent over with their butts facing out, pretending all the Breyer horses had diarrhea, or making the dolls recite *Kids in the Hall* sketches. Helen was a hippie at heart and deeply kind, but nothing made me laugh more than when she would talk in hushed tones about an asshole customer. When she asked if I wanted to babysit her two boys, I said yes immediately.

Unsurprisingly, her kids were as cool as she was. They'd all just moved to Warwick from Bergen County and lived in a sweet house near McEwen Street. Her seven-year-old, Jansen, was a cartoon come to life—he was all red hair, freckles, and boundless energy. Her five-year-old, Ryan, was the sweetest kid I'd ever met—he had big blue eyes and a smile that almost took over his entire face. We mostly played out in the backyard on the swing set; all the kids from the neighborhood would come over when they saw the boys outside, so it was like I was babysitting for five kids at once. They liked science and music, and over the years I always let them stay up a little late to watch *Are You Afraid of the Dark?* and *All That* on Nickelodeon. They never gave me a hard time about going to bed or following their parents' rules about what snacks they could eat. My friends complained endlessly about the kids they babysat, but Jansen and Ryan were easy and cool. Helen's husband, CJ, was a chef, so I always ate like a champion. Even the leftovers were delicious.

My favorite part of the night was when Helen and CJ came home and told me about where they had been. They went to concerts, dinner, house parties. Sometimes they took turns getting drunk; Helen would come in and send CJ down to the basement immediately. "Someone had too much fun tonight." Standing in the kitchen together, we'd laugh about the funniest thing that happened with the kids earlier. They didn't ask me about homework or school like other adults; they wanted to know what I was reading, where I wanted to go after high school, who I hated. I felt like I was being looped into a world where I wasn't a sad loser kid without a mom who lived with her grandparents, but an interesting person with valuable thoughts.

Helen always checked on the kids on her way upstairs. I couldn't remember the last time someone checked to see if I was home, safe, and comfortable. They were kind, loving, fun. I thought about how different my life would have been if I had been born into something so normal. I was on the periphery, but the Truitts always made me feel like I was an integral part of what made family work.

Mostly I was grateful that I didn't have to work at Action Park.

Action Park was one of the most important of all summer initiations for kids in southern New York and northern New Jersey. It was advertised as a water park full of family fun and excitement but was, in reality, a demented, slap-dash horror show built by a conglomerate of *Scooby-Doo* villains, where every ride could end your life. It was also entirely staffed by teenagers. Cory worked there for a summer, but he refuses to talk about it to this day, like a soldier who returned from the war with PTSD.

Everyone knew that Action Park was a death trap, including the parents who dropped their kids off for the day and drove away, to the point where we all referred to it locally as Accident Park. Parents who stuck around could be found at the Stage, watching has-been bands from the eighties perform their singular hits while getting drunk with the teenagers who were supervising the rides between keg chugs. Then they'd all throw themselves into cars and drunkenly weave their way home, sunburned and reckless. I spent most of the money I earned on cassette tapes but always left a little to go to Action Park at least once per summer, which had more per-minute thrills than any movie could offer.

The place was pure mayhem; we survived winter solely to get to the glorious payoff of summer, where we could watch someone drown in the wave pool, break their back jumping from the rope swing, or slice their legs open at the bumper boats.

The prospect of death was an ominous presence from the minute you walked in the park. There, on the right, was a ride so dangerous it had only opened to the public for a month but stood as a legendary symbol of harm: the Cannonball Loop. It was a long black slide with a single loop at the end. The idea was that you would work your way up the rickety wooden staircase that zigzagged behind it until you reached the top, where a stoned teenager would hose you down with water for the lubrication needed to propel you toward the loop, hopefully with enough velocity for you to clear it. The only problem was that most people didn't clear it—most got stuck at the bottom, so many, in fact, that a trap door was cut into it to let them out.

Allegedly.

Others dropped from the top part of the loop and broke their necks or cracked their skulls open.

Allegedly.

The biggest rumor we whispered to each other was that the park sent dummies down to test the ride, and they all slid out onto the rubber mat at the end missing arms and legs.

Allegedly.

The rides that *were* open to the public still contained plenty of chances for dismemberment. The Wave Pool seemed like an innocuous place to take a dip and cool off on a hot summer's day. A giant concrete slab at one end of the pool slapped the water in lazy intervals, creating waves. They weren't big enough to surf but were definitely big enough to drown you if you lost focus for even ten seconds. Someone got sucked under once and died being slapped to death by the thick, concrete slab.

The Tarzan Swing could have been a fun, easy way to enjoy the day. Imagine grabbing a thick rope, swaying through the air, and dropping into a cool pool of water.

A normal person would have invented a ride like this, simple and relaxing.

The demented fucks at Action Park built a ramshackle rope bridge that was as stable as a tightrope walk made of dental floss, attached some frayed lengths of rope precariously to a pole, and made the sign of the cross as legions of children grabbed hold and pushed off. You were lucky if you got to actually hold on to the rope; I mostly saw kids pushing their friends off the edge when they weren't paying attention, and drunk adults with Ray-Ban tan lines losing their grip and sliding down the entire length of rope, skidding to a stop at the bottom with the first two layers of skin missing from their palms. Bless your heart if you tried a back flip or anything fun that you saw in the commercials; I'd seen enough people carted out on stretchers with neck braces to never be that brave.

I would not personally recommend Roaring Rapids, Action Park's answer to riding a cushiony tube down a lazy river. The water was freezing, and the unregulated force of the rapids often upended people right out of the tube. Broken noses were not uncommon as people smashed their faces on the jagged rocks below or met the business end of rocks being chucked by teenage boys floating on tubes in front of you, trying to get your attention. (This is how we flirted in the old days.)

Water slides, typically a lackadaisical affair, took a sinister turn at Action Park. I was too afraid of heights to ever try it myself, but Cory likes to say he almost died on the Kamikaze. One of the main attractions of the water slides at Action Park was that they dropped you from ferocious heights, so much so that a length of rubberized fabric had to be stretched over the first twenty feet or so of each slide to prevent you from flying off the edge as you gained momentum. They made you cross your arms over your chest as you lay down at the top—you know, the way they pose people in coffins. "My face skidded on the rubber!" Cory was very excited. There were several bumps and hills on the slides that caused you to catch air as you rocketed toward the bottom or prayed for the sweet release of death, slamming you back down onto the hard plastic slide over and over again, legs and arms akimbo. I never saw anyone arrive at the bottom feet first with their arms still crossed over their chest as they were positioned when they began; they slid down like rag dolls, sideways or upside down, and crying. Always crying.

Action Park was equal parts water and blood, hubris and neglect. There should have been an EMS attendant at every ride and a blood-borne illness check as you left the park. Having already lived with a man who beat me up on a regular basis, I didn't see the need to flirt with death at Action Park, and I generally kept to the tamer rides. But death comes for us all, and it came for me in the form of the Alpine Slide.

Imagine looking at thousands of feet of ski trails and saying, "You know what this needs? A meandering, solid, concrete half-tube that bakes in the sun all day, where we can send children down at lightning speeds on what amounts to a lunch tray on wheels." The Alpine Slide was colloquially known as the Skin Ripper, the Finger Smasher, and the Alpine Skinless. In 1980, someone genuinely died on the Alpine Slide; he flew off a malfunctioning sled and hit his head on one of the many, many jagged rocks dotting the landscape around the ride. Action Park was so dangerous that even knowing the nicknames and body count, this was the ride I *chose*, the one I thought I had the best chance of surviving intact.

I sat on my scooter at the top of the hill. My feet were next to my butt, my knees bent and almost touching my eyes. My back rounded as I hung on to the steel handle, which was somehow both my steering column and brake. A dead-eyed, monotone teenage boy gave me my instructions so fast he may have been the Micro Machines guy.

"Keepyourhandsinsidekeepyourlegsinsideusethebraketoslow-downhaveagoodtime," he slurred, before giving me a customary shove.

I realized I was going too fast when I hit the first curve. Instead of following the slide, I bounced off the edge, tumbling into the grass. Thankfully, my scooter bounced with me, and I didn't hit any rocks with my head. I picked it up and positioned myself back on the slide, accidentally rolling over my fingers as I tried to gain purchase and get going again. I pushed the steering column to engage the brake, hoping to have a leisurely ride down to the bottom.

Not only did the brake fail to engage, but the kid rocketing toward me from behind couldn't stop, either. He slammed into me full force, again sending me over the edge, this time scraping my shoulder against the concrete slide as we tumbled. I stood up on the grass; once I was sure I had all my fingers and toes, I looked at my arm. A thick, red rope of a burn twisted around from my shoulder to my elbow. It stung and was tender to the touch.

The kid who slammed into me was already back on his scooter and near the bottom.

I decided to forgo the rest of the ride and carried my scooter down the grass as reckless idiots whizzed past me. I wasn't averse to scars, but I was freaked out at the thought of dying in a driving accident before I even had my license. *This is smart*, I thought. *I'm being safe*. Now that I was making my own money, Grandma couldn't prevent me from using it to tempt death all summer.

I ran to Roaring Rapids after I got to the bottom of the slide, dipping my arm in the disease-ridden churn as my inner tube bobbed along. The cold water really felt good on the burn. I was part of it now, the grand scale of insanity disguised as fun, baptized in blood and fear. I had tried to follow the crowd, and now I was done. I went back to Action Park a few times to spend a day outside with friends, but I never went on the rides again.

As I saved my paychecks and faced my first year of high school, I looked at this stage of my life as another hurdle before I reached my ultimate goal: graduating and getting the fuck out of Warwick. At some point, I'd read about Drew Barrymore getting emancipated from her mother and was consumed by the thought that I might one day get to live on my own. I envisioned decorating my walls with Led Zeppelin posters, going to bed anytime I wanted, sitting on the toilet with a good book for hours if I felt like it, and eating pizza for every meal—which is not far off from how I live as an adult. More than anything, I thought that living alone at fourteen years old would bring me the peace and solitude that I had not yet experienced in any iteration of living with my family. I broached the subject with Grandma.

"Drew Barrymore got emancipated from her mom."

I threw myself into the chair in the living room, while Grandma sat on the couch, smoked her cigarette, and flipped through *People* magazine, not reacting to me at all.

I continued. "She lived on her own and was just a teenager."

Grandma lifted her head and stared at me, as if to say "So fucking what?"

"She was just a teenager," I reiterated, "and I work, so . . ." I let the sentence trail off, hoping that Grandma could make the logical leap with me.

"And how, exactly, would you afford an apartment?"

"I have a job. And I'll get another one."

"When would you work if you go to school?" Grandma kept staring at me while she took a long drag.

"I'd keep the schedule I have now," I said enthusiastically.

"So you can pay for rent, electric, gas, garbage, water, heat, and food on your little twenty hours a week?"

". . . Yes." I had no idea what I was talking about.

"That girl is a millionaire. You want to move out on babysitting and toy store money? Be my guest."

"Well, how much does electric cost?" I was determined to make this work.

Grandma tutted, went upstairs. She came back with a stack of envelopes tied in a rubber band from the gray two-drawer filing cabinet in our bedroom. This was the intricate system she used for all her important paperwork—just jam it together and tie a rubber band around it, then throw it in the filing cabinet.

"Here," she said, wrestling an envelope out of the stack. I noted the Orange & Rockland logo as I slid the piece of paper out, then unfolded the bill. In a large font at the bottom, it read: AMOUNT DUE $150.

"That's for one month?" My jaw dropped. It took me two jobs and three weeks to earn $150.

Grandma laughed, picking up the Nintendo controller and restarting her game. "Yep! That'll change your tune, huh?"

Living alone was going to take some time. I resigned myself to high school instead.

High school is a big leap—you're going from the top of the heap to the bottom, the biggest to the smallest at the worst time to make such a change. You're already navigating painful summer growth spurts that leave you feeling like a newborn foal trying to stand up for the first time, and your face is exploding into a psychedelic array of bumps and oil slicks. Your body starts naturally making the kinds of smells you thought only emanated from dumpsters, and for no reason, several times a day, you feel like a soaked sponge. Preteen emotions operate in two modes: happy and sad. Your new teenage emotional life now includes a palette of shockingly unstable hormonal displays: jealousy, rage, deep sadness, happy crying, utter confusion, planetary worries about the hole in the ozone layer, new bras, balls dropping, and, for some reason, wanting to wander through graveyards as the height of romance. Hair takes on Wolfman-like proportions, teeth are wrangled into place, and your skin starts erupting. Then, one day, you have to drag this melting, exploding haversack of viscera into high school, a landscape filled with people who have already surpassed this horror and come out on the other side glistening like a new car.

If you see a teenager in the wild, be gentle. Every single one, even the coolest among them, is navigating the world like a twitching sack of snakes stuck in the molting phase.

Compared to the middle school, Warwick Valley High School was huge. Anxiety set in early about whether I'd have time to get from class to class as I traversed the wide expanse of the hallways in a sea of people. Other kids were thinking about stories from their siblings, replete with eighties teen movie villains dunking their heads in toilets, giving them wedgies, or shoving cow shit through the slots of their lockers. Like every unpopular, maladjusted weirdo before me, I was already accustomed to feeling wildly out of place— I just wanted to make sure I got a seat before the bell rung.

Grandma was worried about me for other reasons. "Jesus Christ, Rene, you should see what she's wearing," she told my aunt, twisted phone cord bouncing against her elbow as she tried to conceal her laughter.

Emboldened by a summer spent reading *Sassy* magazine, thrift shopping, and sewing, I had the perfect outfit in mind for my first day of high school, something that would announce to my fellow classmates that I had zero shits left to give about them and warn the seniors that they were dealing with a wholly unique mother-fucker. I purchased almost thirty neckties at a thrift store bag sale—anything you could fit in a brown paper bag was yours for one dollar—bought a zipper from Dayton's, and spent a full day at my sewing machine dutifully stitching them all together halfway down, letting the pointed ends fly free. In the end, I had concocted a multicolored, technicolor dreamcoat of a tie skirt, stiff at the top for lack of a waistband. I threw on a white T-shirt, some white leggings, and my Converse sneakers. I looked *fucking rad*.

I'd modeled the finished product for Grandma as soon as I completed the final stitch, but she was still shocked when I followed through with wearing it to my first day of high school. "So that's your outfit, then?" Her shoulders shook, a marker of how she geared up for one of her epic howls. "That's my grandchild," she laughed, shaking her head.

In the hallways at school, people stared. Some pointed. *Fuck 'em*, I thought, stomping toward my assigned locker in the basement. *I already live with the meanest person in town.* For the next four years, I was determined to avoid the trap of normalcy and become the art-loving, city-roaming weirdo I knew I was meant to be.

For no good reason other than I thought it looked cool, I had decided to shave my head. My commitment to not giving a fuck what people thought of me grew with every day I walked the halls. I wanted a little ponytail left at the top, and the rest underneath it gone. The only barber in town seemed to cater to old men, and I wasn't sure they'd even let me in the door. Cory became my only option; his friend Lucian, a recent transplant from New York City, had clippers that Cory could borrow.

I sat on the floor in front of my bed while the clippers buzzed to life behind me. "Grandma is going to kill you," Cory said smiling, shearing off the first clump of hair.

"Just concentrate on making a straight line!" I snapped. I knew that he was right. Even though she repeatedly told me that I could do what I wanted to do with my own body, she still held Cory and me to strict ideals that involved not embarrassing her in public.

When he was finished, I stood up as Cory eyeballed a measurement on either side of my ears using his pointer finger. "I think I got it pretty straight," he said proudly.

"You think?!" I ran to the mirror. My cheekbones were more prominent, but I still looked like a Cabbage Patch Kid instead of a cool, heavy metal–loving badass. "It's not really even on the right." I paused. "I guess we can just cut more?"

Cory's eyes lit up. "Okay!"

When Grandma came home from work, I trotted downstairs and walked past her to the kitchen as casually as possible. "Child, what did you do to your head?" I returned to the living room.

"I shaved it." I didn't want to apologize for what I wanted to look like anymore, whether it made Grandma feel bad or not. It was a bit too heavy to carry the burden of my whole race and the respectability politics that ruled Grandma's life. I wanted the freedom of a white kid—to mess up, to go wild, and still have access to a life beyond my teenage mistakes.

Grandma stared at me. "I don't like it."

I stared back. "Well, it's my head, so you don't have to." I was testing out the defiance that I wanted to possess as I moved through the world, except I was starting with the scariest character at the end of the video game level—my grandma. If I could defeat her, no one else stood a chance.

"It certainly is your head," Grandma said, sighing. She was tired from being on her feet all day in the Greenbrier Room. She unbuttoned her shirt halfway, then reached back and unhooked her bra. Her tits dropped like boulders rolling down a hill as she tossed the bra to the far side of the couch. "I guess you can do whatever you want, even if you look like a boy. It's your problem now."

There was a bit of freedom in knowing Grandma didn't like my haircut but there was nothing she could do to change it. I could possess my body in this small way.

———

I wanted to take my new self into the real world, to see how I fit and if I could find like-minded people. New York City seemed like the perfect testing ground; it was the home of the bright, peacock-colored club kids who were sometimes on *Phil Donahue*; CBGB and the punk scene I was starting to discover; and Anna Sui, a favorite of the designers I was beginning to pay attention to in magazines. Most Warwick kids went to the city with their families; they'd come home with reports of seeing the tree in Rockefeller Center or some show at Radio City Music Hall. I didn't give a shit about family fun—I wanted to see the *real* New York City, the one that was a playground for my grandparents and the site of personal transformation for almost everyone I admired.

Grandma drew the line at letting me go to the city alone, where, in her mind, I would instantly be raped, strangled, and mutilated in the middle of Times Square. "It's a disgusting place," she said, screwing up her face. "We left for a reason, you know." It never occurred to me, but Grandma hadn't been back to the city more than a handful of times since she moved to Greenwood Lake. Our city family always came to us. She had completely distanced herself from her roots and was confused that I was now dying to go there.

She agreed that I could go to the Willowbrook Mall. It was one stop away from New York City on the bus but felt safer to my grandma than the thought of me roaming around the East Village on my own.

"I could still get raped and mutilated in a mall," I said matter-of-factly.

"Not likely—you're six feet tall, and you look like a crazy person with that hair," Grandma said, laughing. "You won't be anyone's first choice. Now, which side do you look at when you want to come home?"

I was kneeling on a kitchen chair, hunched over the table, as Grandma stood next to me and pointed to the tiny print on the black-and-white New Jersey Transit bus schedule.

"The other side."

"Right." She flipped over the rectangular tri-folded paper. "Show me what time."

I squinted at the numbers, running my eyes down the list, trying to keep them in line with the places the bus stopped. I pointed at the grid.

"Four forty-five."

"Good. You still biting those nails?" Grandma lifted my finger from the schedule and sucked her teeth in disgust. "A filthy habit. No boys are gonna want to hold your hand if you always have your fingers in your mouth, you know."

"I don't want to hold hands with any boys."

"You're going to get typhus, sucking on those filthy fingers all day."

"What's typhus?"

"Never mind. If you're not home by six p.m., I'm going to assume you've been kidnapped, and if you get kidnapped, well, that serves you right."

I grabbed the schedule from the table and stood up. "I'm six feet tall, and everyone already assumes I'm an adult. I'm not going to get adult-napped." I looked down at Grandma, lightly poking the top of her head. "You're getting a bald spot."

Grandma laughed. "Get the fuck out of here," she said, swatting my hand away. "You have enough money?"

"Yeah. I have a hundred dollars in babysitting money."

"Don't go flashing it around," Grandma said seriously. "Keep your money in your bag, and when you pay for things, don't take it all out at once."

"I knooooooooow," I said, rolling my eyes. She'd been giving me the same instructions forever, even if I was just going to the Grand Union to buy her maxi pads in our cowpoke town.

"I'd tell you to tuck it in your little bra," she said, motioning to my flat chest, "but it would just slide down." Grandma laughed one of her Pillsbury Doughboy laughs, cracking herself up. "Keep your bus fare in your bra," she said, suddenly serious. "If anyone tries to grab you, you know what to do?"

I rolled my eyes again. "Cut his dick off."

"That's right," Grandma said. She pointed at me and tilted her head up to look me in the eye. "If anybody ever puts their hands on you, you cut their pecker right off."

Grandma had been encouraging me to castrate men since I was old enough to know what dicks even were. She'd regale me with tales of her friends from the city who got mixed up with bad men, and that was combined with the threat of street violence, horror movies, and after-school episodes of *Oprah*. The mechanics of this seemed dubious to me; where was I going to carry a knife? Would they just be standing there while I unbuttoned their pants to flop out their offensive member?

Grandma filled the kettle at the sink and popped it on the stove. "Have fun at the mall, baby. Back by six, you hear me?"

I heard her. I smiled and ran upstairs. I was finally going to experience some freedom. I was too excited—it was just a mall, after all. But if I conquered this trip a few times, I might muster the courage to stay on the bus for one more stop and reach my true destination.

The bus stop in front of the Burger King and next to the Chinese restaurant on Oakland Avenue had a small vestibule, but most of us stood waiting near the high wooden planter box instead. When the bus arrived, the door swung open, and I hopped on. Oakland Avenue was the first and last stop of route 197; I was the only one on the bus. The fourth seat back had the most leg room, but it was reserved for people with disabilities, so I wedged myself into the third row.

It took almost two hours to go over the mountain, wind our way around Greenwood Lake, through the woodsy parts of New Jersey where the Real Housewives live, and on to Willowbrook Mall. I listened to my cassette player a little bit but was afraid the batteries would die, leaving me with no music for the way home. I looked out the window instead and thought about how many twists, turns, and potholes I would recognize if I were put in the trunk of a car, assuming the inevitable kidnappers took this exact route.

The mall was okay. It had the same stores as the Galleria, but their head shop had better incense and cloth purses. What I liked most was being alone. In my house and life, solitude was rare. I took my time navigating in any direction I wanted to go, choosing when I was hungry for a snack, and deciding how long I wanted to spend in the record store without being hurried along to Sears. I meandered and relaxed, feeling the day spread before me.

When it was time to get back on the bus, I stood at one of three bus stops. The 197 came through, and I hopped on, but thought to ask, "Is this bus going to Warwick?"

The driver looked at me and motioned for me to stand aside so the other passengers could get through. "One more stop, and that's Port Authority," he said gruffly. "Warwick bus, stand at that one." He pointed to one of the other bus stops across from ours. I thanked him and hopped off the bus, proud of myself for thinking to ask the question but excited by the notion that Manhattan was just twenty minutes and one stop away.

After a few more trips to the Willowbrook Mall, I started staying on the bus and sneaking into New York City. The markers started becoming familiar—the skyline visible across the Hudson River as the bus made the arc that delivered us into the Lincoln Tunnel, the whoosh of sound as we rocketed underwater, the valve release of being poured into Midtown, past the Covenant House, around the blazing-red New Yorker Hotel sign, and into the hot, rank Port Authority Bus Terminal. I followed the other riders off the bus and down the stairs, frantically trying to read signs overhead that pointed me toward the street. I flashed back to Grandma squeezing my hand tight as I left the building. I walked, not knowing where I was going, just to feel like I was part of the humming sea of New Yorkers. The street numbers started going up, but I knew I wanted to go downtown toward the Village, so I crossed the street and walked toward where I had just come from. The post office building had huge pillars and looked more like the White House than our tiny brick building on Main Street in Warwick. It was right across from Madison Square Garden, which I'd seen on TV when the Knicks played.

It felt like I couldn't go a square inch without bumping into something I'd seen, heard, or read about. My mind exploded, every synapse firing at once while I took in how tall the buildings were, how loud the cars honked, how fast the people moved. No one paid any attention to me—they didn't call me weird or ask what planet I came from. I just fit in, an invisible molecule in a larger, more interesting system.

When my friend Leslie and I decided to sneak into the city to see a Jellyfish concert at the Roseland Ballroom, I'd never been to the city at night, but we were confident that we'd be back before anyone could even think to be suspect. Leslie lived in Pine Island; we bonded over our love of heavy metal. She wore black every single day, rotating out a carefully cultivated group of band T-shirts that, if she sold them on eBay today, would make her a few thousand dollars. Leslie was always up for a concert, or anything having to do with getting out of town. We told our wards we were going roller-skating at a rink near the Pennsylvania border. They believed us because we were both good kids, and dorky enough to choose something as old-

fashioned as roller-skating for a fun Saturday night out. I took the
bus from Oakland Avenue, while Leslie drove to the new park-and-
ride near Homestead Village and met me on the bus.

The address for the Roseland was on the ticket; both Leslie and
I knew that the streets of New York were laid out like a grid and
figured we could find out where it was on our own. In the time
before cell phones, we all navigated like Pilgrims. We excitedly
ran through the Port Authority, spilling out the entrance near Strawberry and the Peter Pan bus counters on the Forty-Second Street
side of Eighth Avenue.

New York City at night was a different animal. The buildings
felt taller, as the lights from the windows stretched into the night
sky like stars. Steam poured out of holes in the streets for reasons I
could not fathom, giving everything the feeling of an old black-
and-white movie. Instead of seeing faces, you just felt movement,
like being constantly aware that someone was behind you. The smell
of steaming hot dog carts rivaled the smell of piss as drunk men
rambled out of bars, relieving themselves on any building that was
close enough to conceal them. Sometimes, if you stayed close to
the Port Authority and the Theater District, you'd see the glittering shimmer of a going-out dress, the soft whisper of a camel hair
coat, hair swept into distinctive curls around faces with too much
makeup on. All of this life, this wonder, experienced in a span of
minutes.

I can't remember if it was an all-ages show or if we just talked
our way in. I was used to the doorman dance by now, having wea-
seled my underaged way into a few butt-rock shows at the Chance
in Poughkeepsie, a tiny club where people eventually started getting

stabbed. "I don't drink—I just want to see the show. You can even give me a bracelet so the bartenders know not to serve me." At my full height of six feet tall, most doormen just let me in without asking, assuming I was eighteen or, possibly worse, knowing that I wasn't. It was a hustle, but it was also the truth, and it always worked.

The show started a little late, but we didn't care. We spilled out onto the street with the crowd, and Leslie asked someone what time it was. When I heard 11:30 p.m., my heart sank. The last bus to Warwick was at 12:03 a.m.

We started running. We gave up running after three blocks; I felt like my lungs were going to explode. Instead, we walked very fast, like a couple of grandmas trying to exercise by doing laps around the mall. Waiting at red lights was agony, the clock ticking down.

When we were a block away from the Port Authority, we started running again. "What time is it?" I breathlessly asked someone as we sprinted by. "It's eleven fifty-four p.m."

I stopped short. "Shit. What gate?"

Leslie looked at me. I knew that we could buy tickets on the bus but had no idea which gate the last bus to Warwick left from.

There was a line at the only open booth. We sped past it and right to the front with the full audacity of teenagers who were scared shitless. "I'm sorry, it's an emergency!" I pleaded with the line behind me. "We just have one question!" I turned to the booth agent. "Which gate for 197 to Warwick? Please?" My voice was shaky. I was trying not to cry, not to feel the defeat of watching the bus pull away before it actually happened.

The booth agent, a short Black woman with deep maroon lip-

stick, snapped her gum. She spoke to me without making eye contact. "Gate 403." The farthest away point from the highest side of
the building.

"What time is it?" Leslie asked.

"Just run!" I shouted back.

We rounded the corner to the 400 gates. Small lines of people
splayed out diagonally at each gate marker, but there was no line at
403. That wasn't a good sign.

When we got to the gate, though, the bus was still idling in its
spot.

I ran to the door and jumped on. "One. For. Warwick. Please," I
said to the driver, completely out of breath. I glanced down the long
aisle to see if we would be able to get a seat. That was when I saw
Granddad, sitting in the front seat directly to my left, the light from
the seat lamp shining down on the *New York Post* open on his lap.

I leapt off the bus.

"You have to buy the tickets," I whispered to Leslie.

"You ladies getting on or what?" the driver called out the door.

"My granddad! Is right there! Buy the tickets," I said, shoving
my last twenty dollars in her hand.

I threw the hood of my sweatshirt over my head as I stepped
back on the bus. "She's buying my ticket," I said hurriedly, cinch-
ing my hood so tight I almost couldn't see. With my right hand
out, I felt the seats along the way for balance before throwing myself in the long back seat and slouching down.

The bus jerked into gear just as Leslie reached the back seat.
"Did he see you?" she asked.

"I don't think so. He was reading the paper." The good thing about Granddad working all the time was that he wouldn't be able to pick any of my friends out of a lineup—he'd never met any of them.

The whole bus ride home, I waited for Granddad to fold his paper, walk down the aisle, and ask me what the hell I was doing. But he stayed in the front. I could see the top of his head peeking out over the seat. I didn't take my eyes off it.

As we got closer to Warwick, I had to formulate a plan. I turned to Leslie. "Hey, if I hop off with you at the park-and-ride, can you just give me a lift back to my house?"

"Yeah, totally."

A terrible thought pierced through my brilliant plan. "But then I'll have to get off the bus before him. He might still see me."

"Just pull your hood up and run off again," Leslie said, as if she'd been dodging grandparents on commuter buses for most of her life.

As we cruised into the lot, I readied my hood. When the bus came to a complete stop, I bolted down the aisle and ran off the bus so fast you would have thought I had fire ants crawling all over me. I ran to Leslie's car and leaned on the hood, fully relieved.

Leslie dropped me off right in front of the house. On my way in, I took off my jacket, bundled it into a ball, and threw it on top of a damp pile of leaves under the front steps, just in case Granddad saw the blue plaid print and got suspicious. When I walked into the house, he was just where I expected him to be, sitting at the kitchen table, a can of sardines cracked open with a bottle of Tabasco next to it, and a plate full of crackers to pile it on top of, reading the paper.

"Hey, Granddad," I said cheerily, reaching into the refrigerator for the iced tea pitcher.

"Hey, baby," he replied, looking up.

I went to the cabinet to get a cup. "Sardines, gross."

"You've never even tried one; how would you know?"

I poured my iced tea and sat down across from him.

"You're in late tonight," he said, looking back down at the paper.

"I was out with Leslie. Roller-skating." I surveyed his face to see if there was any reaction, but he was as docile as ever.

"So," he said, turning the page and snapping the paper flat, "did you have a good time in the city?"

I stopped breathing for a few seconds. I thought about lying, but I just caved instead.

"Yeah. Um, it was fun. I went to a concert." I looked at him, but he was still reading the paper, holding a sardine cracker while he chewed. I rushed to fill the silence. "Grandma doesn't know. But we really just wanted to go to the concert. So please don't tell her."

Granddad looked up at me over his glasses, his watery gray eyes glittering under raised eyebrows. "I don't like the idea of you going to the city."

"I know, but I swear this was the first time," I lied. "I never do anything bad. I just really wanted to go to this one thing."

He maintained eye contact with me while he slipped the sardine cracker into his mouth. He crunched the horrid mix of fish flesh for a few seconds, then looked back at the paper. "I don't think we need to tell your grandmother if you don't do it again," he said nonchalantly, as if he didn't have the power of permanent punishment at his fingertips. "It's not really a place young girls should be running around, especially at night." He looked at me again. "You hear me?"

"Yeah. Yes. Of course. Thank you, Granddad," I said as I stood up. I hugged his shoulders and kissed him on the head. "I should probably go to bed now."

He motioned for me to lean down and kissed me on the cheek. "And don't lie to me—I hate liars," he said.

"I never lie," I lied.

17.

I t took nine years, but I finally caught up with God again.

When the Greenbrier Room closed and was converted back to a nuns-only dining room, Grandma took a job at the Mount Alverno switchboards. It was easier than being on her feet for eight hours, but talking to people all day on the phone sent lightning bolts of irritation through her.

"Why are you calling me again?" Grandma was sitting behind her desk in the big, bright, new reception area. I was there to bring her wallet; she had forgotten it and called after school to ask if I would walk it over. I bit my tongue about how Bobby could have done it, considering all he did was sit at home all day. I was leaning over the counter that served as her desk. Sister Mary Francis stood on the other side, waiting patiently. I smiled at her.

"I just answered that. Now, do you want to call back and ask me the same question again in ten minutes, or are we done here?" Grandma laughed into the receiver. "Okay, bye bye." She looked up at me. "All people do all day is *bother* me. Use your common sense!" She wheeled around to Sister Mary Francis. "What do you want, sister?"

The sister's eyes got huge as she stumbled nervously through her question about the chapel.

"I don't know—I have to ask Joe, and Joe is gone for the day already, naturally. You think that man hangs around here a minute longer than he needs to? Can this wait until tomorrow?" Sister Mary Francis nodded her head. "Thank you kindly." Grandma turned back to me and held out her hand. I dropped her wallet in it as the sister walked away.

I was used to seeing Grandma's grade-A ball-busting at home, but this public interaction with the sister was like witnessing a drive-by bullying.

"Why were you so mean to her?" I asked.

"Mean?" Grandma hoisted her thumb over her shoulder. "She'll be back here in ten minutes asking me the same thing—she doesn't know whether she's coming or going. All she does all day is hang out here and annoy me. It's a goddamn nuthouse around here. Right?" She pointed to a sister walking by the desk. "Is it crazy in here all day or what, sister?"

The sister laughed and nodded her head sheepishly while she bustled away.

Grandma laughed and looked at me. "I'm telling you, child. If I get like this when I'm old—"

I cut her off, already knowing how the lyrics went to this particular song. "Put you in a boat and push you out into the ocean," I said, rolling my eyes. "But you know you're already old, right?"

Grandma shooed me away with her hand, using the other to pick up the phone. "Get out of here, you asshole. No, not you, Father Allen." She put her fingers to her mouth and then held them toward me, a kiss in the form of a goodbye wave, before turning her mouth back to the phone. "So what do *you* want?"

Mount Alverno was tucked back from the road, just beyond a low brick wall and a tapestry of maple trees lining the property on Grand Street, and was home to the Franciscan Sisters of the Poor. The majority of the residents were retired nuns; they bustled around in brown, long-sleeved dresses, black shoes, and brown habits, with dark, delicate wooden rosary necklaces finishing the look. It was rare to see them off campus; they had everything they needed, and if they left for any reason, it was to save the souls of people who didn't live in Warwick.

I had started indicating that I might want a car. I already had my permit; you didn't need a car for that since it was just a written test. But my sixteenth birthday was coming up, and I'd be able to get my license.

"You think I have car money?" Grandma said one night, dipping a damp chicken thigh into a bright green Tupperware bowl full of paprika-sprinkled flour. Fried chicken was one of the five dishes she knew how to make, but we rarely had it for dinner; she hated standing over a hot stove getting pelted with pops of grease from the cast-iron pan.

"I can buy my own car," I said. "I just need to make more money."

Most of the kids I went to school with got their parents' hand-me-down cars; boxy Reliant Ks and wood-paneled station wagons they foisted off on their kids while they upgraded to cars with CD players and daytime driving lights. Bubble-shaped Saabs were the used car of choice among the preppy kids. The incredibly wealthy inexplicably got their own brand-new cars, even though half of them ended up wrapped around telephone poles or crashed through onion fields.

I still rode the bus into the city, but I was desperate for more independence. It was never a foregone conclusion that I would ever have a car, hand-me-down or otherwise. Neither Grandma nor Granddad had ever been behind the wheel of a car, so there was nothing to give, and I knew better than to assume there would be a red-ribboned gift of a car waiting for me on my birthday from a woman who made me buy my own bras. Babysitting and the toy store provided enough income to pay for my phone bill and a few trips to the mall, but if I wanted wheels, I had to come up with another plan.

"You could work at the convent—they're hiring in the kitchen, and I can talk to Deneen—GODDAMMIT!" She leapt back and rubbed a spot on her bare arm where the hot grease landed.

"How much do they pay?"

"More than you have." She pushed her glasses up her nose. "You know you have to pay insurance, too, right? It's not just the price of a car. And insuring teenagers is expensive."

"So many teenagers drive; it can't be that expensive."

"You'd be surprised."

Grandma always knew a lot about the world just from paying attention to it, and she talked with the authority of someone who experienced things she never did. This was her other superpower: shitting all over your enthusiasm with her reality bombs.

"Should I call Deneen?"

"Yeah, call her at work tomorrow." She flipped a few pieces over, revealing the bubbly crispness of the side that was already cooked. "Here—come do this." Grandma stepped to the side as I walked up to the stove. "I'm sick of standing here."

Deneen, the kitchen manager, was a family friend. She and Grandma got close from their time in the trenches of the Greenbrier Room. Deneen was tall, with strong freckles and almond-shaped eyes. Her dark skin was always shiningly well-moisturized, and she was the first person I ever met who had a smile that could legitimately light up a room. We looked like we could have been related, except for the fact that she also had enormous boobs—they stuck out in front of her like a natural version of the Jean Paul Gaultier bras featured in Madonna videos. I was still so flat-chested you could have used my torso to measure right angles.

Getting hired in the kitchen was easy; I had to have a meeting with David, the tiny mustached man who was officially the boss, even though Deneen ran the show. I came prequalified; both David and Deneen could rat me out to my grandmother if I ever fell

out of line. The after-school job was explained easily: I was responsible for setting up the dining room for dinner, laying out the
flatware, filling the water jugs, and stacking the clean plates for the
buffet-style dinner. At the end of service, I would collect the dirty
dishes in big gray tubs, bring them to the dish room, stack them in
green racks, spray them down with a high-pressure hose, and push
them through the industrial dishwasher. They came out of the other
side scorching-hot; after letting a full rack cool down, I dried them
with a towel and stacked them in piles again for the morning crew.
It was a damp and steamy job that left my hands simultaneously
wrinkled and callused, but I liked the solitude and easy sense of
accomplishment.

Sometimes I would be responsible for loading the food onto a
cart and bringing it to the different floors of the campus so that the
nurses could dole out meals to the residents. Most of the sisters who
needed to have their meals delivered were bedridden or unable to
get to the dining room.

A few of the more active sisters lived in a large farmhouse across
the driveway from the main building. We had to bring them food,
too, which meant I had to use the tunnel.

To access the tunnel, you would take the elevator from the
kitchen to the basement. The doors opened to a long, dark hallway. Caged lightbulbs hung uselessly down the center of the ceiling every few feet, showcasing the hospital-green walls dulled in
reverse by a distinct lack of sunlight. If you followed it to the end,
you'd come out near the garage, but if you turned left, the tunnel
would come out under the house. I liked going down there; it was
like delivering dinner to Batman.

Sister Rosamaria lived in the farmhouse and often used the tunnel to get around. Originally from Italy, she had a thick accent and a commanding presence, despite her short stature. Her dark hair was cropped short and streaked gray, like a firecracker had exploded on the crown of her head and left a trail of ashes. She wore black soft-soled Reebok sneakers, making it impossible to hear her when she snuck up behind you to poke you in the middle of your back with her knuckle. This was her way of telling me that I had terrible posture, along with frowning deeply and hunching over as a way of mimicking me before giving a wink and scampering away.

One day, Sister Rosamaria exited the elevator just as I was about to wheel my cart full of Ensure and pot roast into it. As I leaned over to hold the door open for her, she narrowed her eyes. "Donyellah. Are you a vir-jean?"

The question took me by surprise, primarily because I had no idea where this line of questioning was going. "Y-yes," I stammered. It wasn't embarrassing to admit that I hadn't had sex, but it was uncomfortable to be talking about it with a feisty, unpredictable nun.

"Ah! Good girl!" She clapped her hands once in place of punctuation and started walking toward the chapel, even though she was still talking. "You a vir-jean, you become nun."

I laughed nervously. "Probably not."

This made no more sense than the sex advice I got from Grandma. When I was nine, she casually told me that I should never get married, but I should sleep with as many people as possible before settling down.

Repeat: I was nine.

To my knowledge, the only person Grandma had ever had sex with was Granddad; like me, Grandma didn't really care much for dating in her teen years. Do you know what it's like to get sex advice from a septuagenarian? It involves calling Madonna a hussy every ten seconds and is often wildly contradictory to their own experience.

Aside from the odd crush, I didn't think about sex. The most I could muster was how nice it would be to hold hands with someone in a graveyard, which, for some reason, was the height of romance to me. My body still felt foreign to me; it wasn't a source of pain anymore, but it wasn't a source of pleasure, either. I still grappled with the instability of sleep paralysis and insomnia, and was battling persistent lethargy that Grandma chalked up to "just being a teenager." I was still surrounded by whiteness and hadn't yet learned that I was beautiful in a different way.

There was also the question of Luke. Molestation isn't rape, but I'd still been pushed beyond my sexual boundaries before I even knew what my sexual boundaries were. In the eyes of God and the world, I fell somewhere in the chasm between virgin and sex.

But that didn't stop Grandma, or Sister Rosamaria, from telling me what to do. "You a vir-jean!" Sister Rosamaria shouted over her shoulder. "One day, you live with me!"

A few days later, as I was filling water pitchers in a half-full dining room, Sister Rosamaria walked in. "Ah!" she said loudly as she walked over to me. She grabbed my hand and spun me around. "Every-wan! Donyellah is a good girl! She a vir-jean! She's coming to live with us!" she shouted. Every head in the room turned toward us, and a blanket of silence fell over the room. I smiled nervously while Sister Rosamaria stood next to me, the top of her head barely reaching my shoulder.

I felt my face grow hot as I tried to think how I was going to extricate myself from this virgin-obsessed stalker. I stood there and smiled as the sisters went back to eating, ignoring me as if to say "So what? We're all virgins, get in line."

When she let go of my hand, Sister Rosamaria turned to me, winked, and said, "You think about it, ah? You think."

My virginity became a weird inside joke for Sister Rosamaria and quickly fell to shorthand as she rushed around doing her chores. "You still ah? Ah?" she'd say, pointing down to my waist. It didn't feel like sexual harassment; it felt like I was interacting with the world's randiest grandparent. Other sisters would clock us as they walked by; when Sister Rosamaria was out of earshot, they'd often grab my forearm and whisper, "You should be canonized for having to deal with her."

18.

recognized the pulsing blue and red lights through my bedroom curtains and had a brief flashback to Ackerman Road. That was the last time I'd seen police lights up close, until now.

Cory had always run toward every possible bad idea with open arms. He cracked his two front teeth into a perfect V-shape flipping over his handlebars after riding his bike down the steepest hill in town on a dare. He flicked matches at anything not bolted down just to see what would burn, like an arsonist Johnny Appleseed. Cory didn't ever think about consequences—only the biggest laugh, the most immediate rush. This is part of the reason we didn't connect—we had different motivations, and the idea of jeopardizing the future for anything in the present was alien to me.

The train tracks ran through the middle of town, and they were the first place Cory thought to go after finding out his friend Keith had snuck two bottles of Mad Dog out of the house. They grabbed two more friends, and the four of them set off down the tracks. Cory, Justin, and Chucky had split a bottle between them, which was plenty for them to each get blisteringly drunk. Keith had almost an entire bottle to himself; when he reached the bottom of the bottle, he started a rotation of puking and passing out. Even in their drunkest state, Cory and the guys were scared enough to start dragging one another back down the tracks toward town. Keith was fully passed out in the road by the time they reached South Street. Someone must have called; the cops came, and then an ambulance to take Keith to St. Anthony's, where he was treated for alcohol poisoning. Cory, Justin, and Chucky were each brought home in squad cars. I peeked through my bedroom curtains as Grandma went out to talk to the cops. They were all standing next to the squad car; Cory was leaning on Grandma with his full weight, crying uncontrollably. She calmly talked to the officer and put her arm around Cory's waist to steady him. Everyone got warnings, but no one was arrested. As Cory and Grandma made their way into the house, I ran downstairs.

"Is he okay?" I asked. Cory couldn't hold himself up.

"Get out of the way, child," Grandma said, impatient to drag Cory into the house. I closed the front door behind him and followed as she pushed him into a chair at the kitchen table.

"What's wrong with him?" I asked. Cory's arms were crossed

on the table; his forehead rested on them as he cried, drips of snot and drool snaking their way to the floor beneath him.

"He's drunk, numb nuts," Grandma said. "Drinking with his goddamn friends on the train tracks like a bunch of idiots." She was filling the kettle; she put it on the stove, then grabbed the jar of Folgers and a mug. Cory, his head still hanging down, winced when she loudly dropped the teaspoon into the mug and slammed it on the table in front of him.

"Why are you making him coffee?" I asked, feeling my anger rising. Shouldn't she be furious by now? Shouldn't she be yelling in his face?

"To sober him up."

"I'm sorry," Cory slurred. "I'm sorry, I'm sorry."

Grandma rolled her eyes. "Oh, shut up. I know you're sorry. You're gonna be even sorrier when you wake up tomorrow." She walked over and started rubbing Cory's back, then looked at me and motioned with her hand. "Go get a towel."

I couldn't believe my eyes. Cory came home blind drunk, in a police car, *driven by the police*, and she was rubbing his back? This was the same woman who once told me that if I kept falling asleep with the overhead bedroom light on and running up the electric bill she would end my actual life.

"Um, I'm sorry—why? Why should I get him a towel and be nice to him? He's drunk!" I felt like every capillary in my body was about to explode. This was a situation ripe for lifetime punishment, and she was scurrying around like Mary fucking Poppins instead of burying his body in the backyard. I wasn't interested in drinking. I'd seen enough after-school specials to understand that underage drinking always ended in car accidents, sexual assaults, or general life-ruining shame. Plus, no one that I hung out with drank. A girl named Stefanie who Alexis, my closest friend, and I hung out with sometimes brought a six-pack of Zima to a birthday party over the summer; I took one home to try in the privacy of my own room. After turning the bottle over in my hands a few times, I stashed it under my bed and tossed it out on trash night. I had fully bought into the idea that one sip could ruin my life, or at least ruin my chances of getting out of Warwick.

"Keep your voice down, Dani," Grandma whispered tersely. "He's drunk. And who knows how long those jerks were drinking before coming home."

"He didn't come home—he was brought home. BY THE COPS."

"Goddammit, Dani, go upstairs," Grandma hissed. The kettle boiled; she finished stirring the coffee and brought it over to Cory, whose sobs quieted as he took tentative sips.

"This is bullshit!" I shouted. Cory jumped as if he had just been electrocuted, then started crying again.

"Go upstairs, goddammit!" Grandma was shouting now, too, which only caused Cory to grab his head in his hands and wail loudly.

I stomped upstairs to my room. I tried to slam the door, but it just whispered along the high-pile carpet.

About an hour later, I heard Grandma ushering Cory upstairs, talking mostly to herself while he gave the odd grumble in return. I listened through my bedroom door. "Let's air it out, because you know all that alcohol coming out of your pores is gonna stink," she said, opening a window. She must have brought a paper bag up with them; I heard the distinctive *pop!* as she snapped it open. "If you have to upchuck, do it in this bag here, okay?" She was talking loudly, the way Americans do when they travel to other countries, as if loudly saying something in English is the same as learning Spanish or French. His sneakers fell to the floor with a thud as she pried each one off. I could already hear Cory snoring by the time she left the room.

I opened my door and chased after her down the stairs. "So he's really not going to be punished for this?"

Grandma sighed, easing down onto the couch and lighting a cigarette. "There's no use reasoning with a drunk person, Dani. I learned *that* from your grandfather."

I felt confused. "What do you mean?"

"Your grandfather. He drinks, always has. Drank away our chance to buy a house, drank away our chance to do anything, really," she said, waving her hand in the air like she was swatting a fly. She sounded tired and continued talking to the air instead of looking at me. "He still drinks. Not as much. He thinks I don't know. But you can smell it on them." She waved her hand toward the ceiling. "Now this one starts."

I looked at her. She was slumped on the couch, staring at something years in the past. The skin on her face was pulling down toward her neck, ending in a pool of wrinkles. She closed her eyes, while I stood there, shocked. Granddad always had a few beers when our family visited from the city, but we didn't have any alcohol in the house. He did work at a bar, but he never seemed to come home drunk, not in the way that I saw in movies—he wasn't loud, he didn't stumble over things or fall down. I looked at Grandma. What else didn't I know? Was this her way of protecting me—just keeping me in the dark? For a moment, my world wobbled like a top about to fall. She was more adept at being a parent than I had ever realized or given her credit for.

I still felt like Cory was an asshole. Getting drunk on the railroad tracks was such a 1920s hobo-with-a-bindle, lame-ass move. It bothered me that he could be so cavalier, while Grandma held me to a different standard of respectability. I was starting to see cracks in her tough façade, but it felt intentional—like she was showcasing her vulnerability because I was getting older and had earned the right to see it.

But I was also worried. If alcoholism ran in our family, was this just the beginning of the end for Cory? "What if Cory chokes? Like the lady from the Mamas and the Papas?" My newfound interest in the 1960s lent itself well to situations like this, where I could whip out a factoid I'd heard on VH1.

"He's not going to choke, Dani," Grandma said, her eyes still closed. "He's going to sleep, and maybe upchuck. I'm tired, child," she said, opening her eyes and grabbing the TV remote next to her. "Leave me alone."

I went back upstairs and poked my head into Cory's room on the way to mine. He was facedown on the bed, fully clothed, snoring. I left his door open. I left mine open, too, so I could hear him breathing. Just in case.

Grandma usually worked on Tuesdays, but one day when I came home from school, she was sitting on the couch, sponging her face with a wad of tear-soaked tissues. I'd never seen her cry before. Not like this.

I was scared to walk over, not quite sure I could handle whatever elicited this reaction from her. I dropped my bag near the TV and walked over to her, kneeling down to try to meet her gaze.

"What happened?" I asked.

"My best friend is dead," Grandma said, sobs breaking open a space between every word.

Patsy had been hit by a drunk driver while backing out of her driveway that morning. I instantly flashed to moments of her—red bouffant grazing the roof of her car while she drove us to the mall, eating pancakes at Perkins, drinking coffee at the All Seasons Diner, in Grandma's kitchen on Jersey Avenue. She was there for my entire life, an extension of Grandma. She was also the first and only person Grandma was likely to spend time with—I never saw her reach out to other people to just get a cup of coffee or go shopping. They spent 90 percent of their time together laughing, especially after Nana Dar moved to Florida; it's possible they kept the serious conversations away from us kids, but whenever we were around, they were always hunched over, complaining about how they were going to pee their pants. Patsy was the beating heart center of Grandma's joy.

Grandma was inconsolable until Granddad came home. She must have called him at work; he was home before the sun went down, which never happened. I floated up and down the stairs quietly, finding excuses to drift in and out of the kitchen while trying to examine this new way my grandparents were interacting with each other. It was like a curious theatrical production had sprung up in our living room. Granddad was bringing Grandma tissues; Grandma was lying on Granddad's lap, still crying; Granddad was rubbing her shoulder. Before Luke, before bodies became dangerous, I used to make Grandma and Granddad kiss. "Kiss her!" I'd shout, jumping up and down and clapping my hands. They'd laugh as they pecked each other on the lips. "Now kiss *him*!" They entertained me a few times before declaring it was enough.

"What's wrong with you, ya pervert?" Grandma would laugh.

Looking at them now, I realized love wasn't something you could perform but something you felt together.

For months after Patsy died, Grandma couldn't get off the couch. She went to work, came home, and watched TV in the dark until she fell asleep. I forgot what her laugh sounded like.

We didn't put up a Christmas tree that year. It usually went up in early December; Bobby or Granddad would drag the box out from the closet under the stairs, take the green plastic frizz out of the box, and pop the poles together. Cory and I pulled apart each branch, spreading them the way a real tree would look, while Grandma directed us from the couch. We threw stringy tinsel on it while Grandma told us the story of each ornament. "You made this in preschool," she said to Cory, hanging a round piece of cardboard with gold spray-painted macaroni on it. The multicolored bulbs rested on some of the branches, hot to the touch. It was a wonder the house never burned down.

Sometime around the third week of December, I asked Grandma if we were going to put up a tree. I was really asking whether we were going to have Christmas; it wasn't a big family event, but it was something to look forward to. We called all the family in California, and I was still young enough to have some surprises under the tree, even if I no longer believed in Santa Claus.

Grandma rolled over. She'd been lying on the couch, the TV throwing light and shadows on her face. "I don't feel like Christmas this year, Dani," she said into the couch cushion, her back to me. "Watch whatever you want on the TV. I'm going to sleep."

I went upstairs and lay on my bed in the dark. I didn't feel like Christmas, either. There was something about seeing Grandma's grief that helped me identify my own.

I didn't have a language for it, but the lethargy I had been feeling was depression. None of the things that brought me happiness worked anymore—not music, or painting, or reading. If you sliced our house in half like a dollhouse, you'd see me and Grandma, in different rooms but stacked on top of each other, both of us lying down with our grief. Grandma's body mirrored mine as we each stayed on the couch or in bed, her pain echoing my own pain. I couldn't stop thinking about Luke, and Mom, and all the ways they each hurt me. I couldn't talk to Grandma about how I was feeling, because I didn't know how to describe the way I felt, like all my thoughts were a giant blob of dough in a colander that I had to force through the holes with great effort just to take a shower or do my homework. Maybe Grandma would remember her own grief, so she could understand all the times I just wanted to let the dark slip over me, to just sleep, and sleep, and sleep.

A few months after the holidays, Grandma started feeling better. There were more days when she sounded like herself again, and, most surprising, she booked a trip to take Cory and me to California.

Sweetie Pie had moved to Sacramento a few years before, joining Aunt Connie and her husband, Uncle Glen, so we hadn't seen her in a while. Uncle Glen was stationed there in the military; when Sweetie Pie got old enough to retire, it somehow made more sense for her to move across the country than it did for her to land upstate near us. She always visited us when she lived in New York City; this was the first time I was in her home, instead of the other way around.

This was a big trip for us. Grandma tucked away tips, tax returns, and anything extra for years in order to bring me and Cory with her on this trip to California. She did it herself and made a point of reminding me of that while we sat in the travel agent's office: "Your granddad didn't pay for any of this—I wanted to see my family, so I paid for it." We were wedged into uncomfortable wooden chairs in front of an expansive desk, waiting for the travel agent to come back from the printer. I could see our laundromat out the window as I wondered why Grandma felt the need to tell me this. It wasn't a secret to me that she paid for almost everything we ate, did, or possessed; she never shut up about it.

I was still afraid of heights and flying, but no one was as nervous as Grandma. We got to the airport fifteen hours before our flight took off, which gave her a smooth thirteen hours to fidget and ask if I thought anything would go wrong with the flight. She packed enough luggage for any possibility—if a snowstorm touched down in Sacramento, we'd be ready. She insisted on overseeing Cory and me as we packed, even though my plan was to bring the same T-shirts and cutoff jeans I had worn all summer in Warwick. My suitcase could have fallen out of the cargo hold and I wouldn't have missed a beat for the entire two weeks we were gone.

Grandma was excited to visit her mom, but she was less excited about Sweetie Pie seeing my current hairdo. "You need to brush whatever is left of your hair over that shaved part," she instructed as soon as we got to Aunt Connie's house. "And don't wear one of those *outfits*, either—wear something normal, with no holes or tears or rips or paint on 'em." Before we got in the car, I parted my hair in the middle and combed it down to frame my face. It covered the shaved part of my hair underneath; I looked like a tan Emo Philips.

"Mom might surprise you, Carole," Aunt Connie said to my grandma when she picked us up from the airport at the start of the trip. Her driver's seat was pushed so close to the wheel that I wondered how she could navigate around her chest. We talked on the phone every weekend, but I'd only met Aunt Connie twice before, when I was a baby and they came back to New York for visits. She had always been short, but she seemed positively tiny now that Cory and I were six feet tall. Her salt-and-pepper hair was short and natural, and she still wore her signature red lipstick. Grandma was in the passenger seat, looking out the window.

"I know. We talk on the phone," Grandma said.

"But it's different in person. I just want to prepare you, Carole. It's very upsetting in person."

This was the other reason we were here, the real reason, the one I overheard in phone conversations without ever having anything explicitly explained. The low-tone mention of Alzheimer's, the way Grandma wondered if Sweetie Pie should still live on her own. I had the feeling we were there so that Grandma and Aunt Connie could make a big decision together, something that was hard to do when you were three thousand miles apart.

Sweetie Pie's apartment was in the lower level of a small complex; judging from the amount of motorized scooters parked in the walkway, most of the people who lived there were around her age. Her place was filled with books, photos, crocheted blankets from her sister that were similar to the ones we had at home, and records. It was elegant but cozy. The largest wall in her living room was covered with framed family photos. The only pictures we had hanging on our walls at home were the three senior portraits of my mom, aunt, and uncle, all in decreasing degree of afro as each graduated. I walked over for a closer look while Sweetie Pie bustled around the kitchen, her hair in the same soft curls I'd always remembered.

"Are these from Jersey Ave?" I asked, pointing to a frame on the wall of three autumn leaves pressed under glass.

"Yes, Dani, they are," Sweetie Pie said. "Do you remember picking those with me?" She was smiling as she walked over slowly.

I remembered. The simplicity of hunting for the brightest colors on the most crisp day. Sweetie Pie always had an innate patience

with us, a slow-honeyed southernness that showed us a peek of her
Virginian roots. She had that thing that people called "effortless
elegance"—she looked comfortable and cool even then, wearing a
bright blue skirt, a light blue button-down, and a black ribbon tied
in a bow at her neck. A delicate beige cardigan was draped over her
slim shoulders. I was a foot taller than her and constantly felt the
urge to grab her in a powerful hug. Her sentimentality rivaled
Grandma's hardness—I couldn't believe that this serene, delicate
woman raised such a tough taskmaster of a kid. I was starting to
see that between Aunt Connie's femininity and Sweetie Pie's kindness, Grandma was kind of an outlier herself, sharing with me our
insistence on being independent and doing things our own way.
She was able to grow into who she was because she knew her mother
loved and respected her no matter what. That may be the unseen
benefit of growing up with motherly kindness. It was difficult to
accept that this existed in my family, too, that mothers in my direct lineage could be so outwardly tender.

Sweetie Pie patted my shoulder and walked back to the kitchen.
Grandma and Aunt Connie were trying to help, but she shooed
them out. Cory was splayed out on the couch, bored out of his
mind and not even trying to hide it. I turned back to the leaves.
We had pictures in our photo albums from all the times she visited
when I was small; I remembered her so vividly. But the leaves
threw me off-balance emotionally—no one ever told me full stories about our family, and there was so much about my own life
that I didn't understand. We weren't sentimental—Grandma told
stories about her childhood only if I asked, and never with an air
of importance. Sweetie Pie's walls were filled with memories from

top to bottom—pictures of all her grandchildren and their kids, scrawled pictures with shaky letters made with chubby little preschool hands, school photos of Cory and me that Grandma diligently sent out every year. It was my lineage filling these walls, the way I was connected to something bigger than my own small, erratic family.

She brought the glasses of orange juice over to the coffee table, and I sat down to join everyone. I took a sip and winced. Something tasted wrong. It was orange juice, but more sour. It tasted like the juice had gone bad. I looked at Cory and whispered, "Does this taste weird to you?"

He took a huge gulp. "Nope."

I tried another sip and handed the glass to Aunt Connie. "Can you taste this?" My main worry was that Sweetie Pie, in her forgetfulness, was drinking juice past its freshness date.

Aunt Connie took a sip and started laughing. "Gimme that glass!" she said to Cory, reaching out for his half-empty cup. She brought both of our cups into the kitchen and poured them down the sink. "Mother, you can't serve the children *vodka*," she said sternly. Sweetie Pie, apparently a lover of screwdrivers, had mixed a pitcher of them for herself and then forgot.

"Tell me, how old are you again?" Sweetie Pie asked as I sat on the couch.

"I'm fifteen."

"Ah, lovely. And you're Robin?" Her eyes were focused on something in the past, never quite coming into view.

"No, Mother, this is Robin's daughter, Dani," Aunt Connie chimed in.

I looked at Aunt Connie in the kitchen and laughed a little. Cory was cracking up. We were focused on the hilarious fact that we'd just been served a mixed drink by our great-grandmother. Then I looked at Grandma. She was sitting on the couch, patting Sweetie Pie's hand, tears streaming down her cheeks.

The shelf above my bed at Aunt Connie's was loaded down with stuffed animals. The room itself was crammed with fabric, yarn, new and computerized sewing machines, and various craft projects in progress. Aunt Connie was always making things; when we talked on the phone, we talked about patterns and textiles. The way I dressed was the bane of my grandma's existence, but Aunt Connie thought it was cool that I reconfigured outfits out of thrift store clothes. She was the first person who thought I could make a living as a fashion designer, or that I should at least try.

Aunt Connie's house was a sleek one-level beauty, filled with things collected during her and Uncle Glen's years of traveling the world with the military. The sunken living room was home to a sick sound system; there was an old picture of Sweetie Pie sitting in the Eames chair with a pair of headphones and a glass of wine. The garage was strictly Uncle Glen's domain, crammed with the electronic equipment he tinkered with in retirement. As the kids moved out, they slowly turned the bedrooms into offices and crafts rooms.

The neighborhood was a sleepy subdivision, but I'd watched *Gleaming the Cube* enough times to know that was where skaters were most likely to be hanging out. I walked out to the kitchen, where Grandma and Aunt Connie were sitting, trading photos from a huge pile spread out on the table.

"Look at this one of your grandmother, Dani," Aunt Connie said, handing me a black-and-white picture. "Look at the size of that forehead." She laughed, turning to Grandma. "Look at your big ol' head, Carole."

Grandma tilted her head up and looked at the pictures through the bottom of her glasses. "Aw, that was at the park on One Hundred and Thirty-Third Street. Remember taking Colin and Michelle there when they were babies?"

I normally lived for this—sifting through photos and learning about my family through photos. But I was on a mission.

"Aunt Connie, do you have any skate parks here?"

She looked up at me thoughtfully. "I think there's a park down the street where the kids play?"

Grandma looked at her. "She's looking for a park where she can stare at white boys on skateboards, Connie."

My face grew hot with anger. I couldn't believe she knew or that she would rat me out so quickly.

"Oh, we don't have any of those," Aunt Connie said. They both laughed and went back to sorting photos as I stormed out of the room.

Our next stop was Aunt Rene's house. For the past year or so, Aunt Rene had made her living by running a daycare out of her house, and her husband, Gayland, worked for Sony. Aunt Rene and Gayland had relocated from San Francisco after their son, Jordan, was born, and moved to Davis, a hippie-tinged college town twenty minutes west of Sacramento. Jordan was a curly-haired, almond-eyed toddler, and completely adorable. We'd only been in the house for an hour before we already had a game: he'd ask me to lie down on the couch with my hair hanging over the edge, then he'd sneak up, play nice, and pull my hair as hard as he could, collapsing into a pile of giggles.

"Dani, cut it out—don't teach him that," Grandma said. She'd been agitated since the moment we arrived. At the moment she was rooting around for a pot in the kitchen.

"Ma, we're already making dinner. What do you need another pot for?"

"What does it matter to you?" Grandma sniped.

Aunt Rene left the room, walked down to her bedroom, and closed the door. I could hear her talking to Gayland but couldn't make out what she said. It had been like this the whole day—Grandma nitpicking Jordan's nap time, passive-aggressively commenting on the liquid hand soap in the bathroom, making snide comments about how Aunt Rene never learned how to cook. This trip was the first time anyone in our New York family was meeting Gayland and Jordan, and Grandma was deflating that excitement every chance she got.

I was surprised. I figured that Grandma would be happy to see her daughter, the one who didn't cause her any trouble and actually seemed to be really cool and accomplished. But all of those things seemed to have the opposite effect. Aunt Rene was successfully living life on her own terms, so Grandma whittled her down, chose only to see her through the lens of her biggest sin—she was happy, despite or because of leaving our family behind.

Their bickering persisted, even on the day we all drove to San Francisco. Aunt Rene and Gayland rented a minivan to fit all of us. Despite Grandma's back-seat driving during the entire hour-and-a-half trip, Aunt Rene remained excited to show us where she used to live, all of the places she worked and loved. Her energy was infectious as she described old apartments she shared in the colorful dollhouses that dotted the city, the building where she saw the Grateful Dead play every New Year's, the giant rainbow flag that flew over the Castro, the place that had the best burrito in that neighborhood. Looking at San Francisco through her eyes, I saw a city rife with possibility and excitement.

By midday, everyone needed a break from each other, especially Grandma and Aunt Rene. Eager to get some alone time with us, Aunt Rene volunteered to take Cory and me to Haight-Ashbury while Grandma hung back with Jordan and Gayland. I was in the midst of a serious everything-hippie-and-Led Zeppelin phase and couldn't wait to walk around the famed street I'd read about in so many descriptions of the 1960s.

"Lord, I needed a break," Aunt Rene said, rubbing her eyes.

"Yeah, Grandma is kind of a pain in the ass," Cory said, handling a turquoise-flecked glass pipe before catching Aunt Rene's eye and putting it down.

"Try living with her," I chimed in.

"I *did*." Aunt Rene laughed, and we rounded the corner onto the Haight. "Do you ever talk to your mother?" She was inquisitive but not pushy, and just seemed genuinely curious.

"Yeah," Cory said, "sometimes."

"Do you talk to her?" I asked. They were so different; I almost forgot that they were sisters.

"Sometimes. I don't really have anything nice to say to her after what she did to you kids. Look—we're here!" It was jarring to think that someone else thought Mom was wrong to leave us behind. Grandma always made her feelings known, so much so that I didn't feel there was any room for me to have an opinion of my own about what had happened. Aunt Rene really wanted to know what we felt. I felt momentarily cheated—of all the women in my family who could have raised me, why did I have to end up with the most stubborn one?

Years later, Aunt Rene told me that she had considered getting custody and moving us to California with her. I thought about her, in her early thirties, managing record stores, willing to give up Grateful Dead concerts and parties in the park to take care of us. It seemed impossible that someone aside from Grandma, who was always in our lives, could love us enough to even think about such a selfless act.

The Haight was dirtier than I imagined; teenage gutter punks stretched across the sidewalks holding signs and begging for change, their black denim and leather outfits coated with grime, dreadlocked and filthy. Most of the stores we went into looked like they were still being run by the people who originally opened them decades earlier. The tourist trap stores had posters of Jimi Hendrix and Jerry Garcia and blacklight posters of psychedelic mushrooms. Music

pumped out of doorways, and people sat in windows smoking
in their apartments above. I was in heaven as we dipped into a
secondhand store.

As we moved down the aisles, I pulled out dresses with flower
designs, old pairs of jeans, shoes with chunky heels. My eyes caught
the pattern on a pair of pants. The white spandex was decorated
with wavy brown and orange horizontal lines that covered each
leg. Huge bell bottoms flared at the hems in floaty circles. They
were disgusting, and as soon as I held them in my hands I knew I
would be buying them. I showed them to Aunt Rene.

"I'm getting these."

"Will they even fit? You're very tall."

I held them up to my waist. The bell bottoms started at my
knees and ended at my calves.

"Yeah. I'll just put a skirt over them."

Aunt Rene burst out laughing. "Child, you definitely have a
mind of your own."

She held out her arm as we approached the counter and took
out her wallet.

"No, I can pay for them myself—I have a job."

"I do, too." Aunt Rene winked at me as she handed the cashier
a twenty.

"Thanks," I said, feeling spoiled for the first time in my life.

———

We capped off the trip to San Francisco with a drive through Pa-
cific Heights. Gayland was trying to point out all of the big houses

overlooking the bay and tell us which ones were used for movie sets, but it was hard to concentrate over Grandma and Aunt Rene's hushed fight about everything from how Rene was feeding Jordan to Grandma's discomfort with sitting in the car for so long.

The tension that had been palpable for days finally broke. Jordan was sleeping in his car seat, so they were trying not to be too loud, but it was easy to tell that they were sniping at each other from the clipped way they were talking. Why did Grandma have to be like this, even on vacation? All day she complained—her feet hurt when we got to Fisherman's Wharf, so she wasn't able to tour the pier. She only wanted to eat at chain restaurants. She didn't want to go to Haight-Ashbury. Golden Gate Park was too big and there was nothing to do. It took too long to drive everywhere.

I shrunk down in my seat, unable to bear the sound of them fighting in my vicinity but unable to escape. I kept my ears perked up, though; in all the time I'd spent with her, I'd never heard someone fight back with Grandma . . . and win.

I heard Aunt Rene asking Grandma if she would rather just go back to Aunt Connie's house, if she could stand to admit that she wasn't right about everything, if she could back off and let her raise her own child her own way. Usually, when Grandma was done making her point, she just left the room, not giving anyone a chance to chime in or give their perspective. In the car, she was trapped.

Aunt Rene had already taught me about music, cities, and dicks. But she also illuminated all the ways that Grandma was stubborn, all the ways she could be right about her own life and wrong about mine. It was possible to get away and live life on your own terms. It was possible to survive.

19.

Dani, come down here and *tell me what's wrong.*"

I couldn't tell if I'd passed out or just fallen asleep, but I opened my eyes and looked outside, trying to tell the time by the position of the sun. It was dark outside. I'd missed the whole afternoon.

I was supposed to be living my best teenage life—I was turning sixteen soon, had jobs that weren't too awful, was saving money. But for months, I had been coming home after a day of pretending that I could handle my feelings, going up to my room, and crying for hours. I had been struggling with these feelings since I last saw Mom, but lately they had descended over my whole life. I would lie down on my back and stare at the ceiling as a heavy feeling wrapped itself around my heart, creeping in like a fog the way it always did. I might feel fine one day, but then, out of nowhere, I thought about how ugly I was, or how unintelligent, or uncreative. I thought about Mom. I thought about Luke.

Once school went on summer break, I spent most of my time alone. I went to work and babysat, but I wasn't reaching out to friends. I don't remember going to the movies, or the mall, or even meeting anyone for a slice.

When my phone rang, I was a little surprised; for most of the school year, I had stopped having the hours-long conversations with friends that used to fuel my days. I reached over to pick it up without looking at it.

"Danielle! Are you coming?" Alexis was smarter than most of our teachers and crafted every opportunity possible to help the chances of getting out of Warwick, like playing soccer and joining student government. She sounded like she was in a crowd of people, which was odd—she was more likely to be found at home studying on any given night, including weekends. But one of our friends, Vicki, was having a party, she said. Vicki was the kind of friend I sat with at lunch but never called.

"I don't think so. I have cramps," I lied.

"Come on. Take an Advil and come to the sleepover."

"I really can't."

"We'll come pick you up!" Alexis was always the first person to take no for an answer; her insistence was completely out of character.

"No. I can't."

"Come on, Danielle!" Vicki shouted in the background.

Alexis sighed into the receiver. "We're trying to throw a surprise sweet sixteen party for you, you jerk." She sounded angry. I choked back the golf ball of tears stuck in my throat. Thinking about leaving my bed made me feel queasy, but I'd never had anyone throw me a birthday party before. Their kindness shocked me, and the fact that I couldn't possibly drag myself out of the house made me feel more depressed. They were right there, showing me how much they cared about me, and I couldn't stop myself from wallowing enough to accept it.

A few months earlier, instead of just thinking about suicide, I had thought I might actually try it. Movies made it look easy, but suicide was not an easy thing to do.

I didn't want it to be messy; I thought about Grandma having to clean up brains or puke, and smiled a little thinking that she'd be more upset about the mess I left behind than she would be about the fact that I had killed myself. In the Keanu Reeves movie *Permanent Record*, his best friend threw himself off a cliff, but Warwick was a mercilessly flat place. People seemed to like taking pills, but which ones? Our medicine cabinet was empty of medication, and the strongest things we had in the house were Tylenol, nail polish remover, and a five-year-old bottle of Care Free Curl.

I hated the sight of blood, but cutting my wrists was the only viable option.

Sitting on my bed, I reached into my book bag and took out my compass. The pointy tip was sharp enough to accidentally stick me a few times; it would be fine for a practice run. I wanted to be sure I could handle hurting myself.

I held the point against my left wrist and paused. Should I stab it in, or draw it over a length of skin until I hit a vein? I pressed down. It didn't matter how I opened up my skin.

It felt like a wasp sting; then a small bead of blood rose to the surface as I pulled the compass away and dropped it on the floor. I stared at my wrist. There was no gushing, not even a drip. Just a small maroon dot slowly growing against the pale underside of my wrist.

I licked my thumb and wiped it away. A small dot of blood took its place. I licked and wiped again, then held my thumb against it. When I pulled my thumb away minutes later, there was no blood in sight.

All I wanted to do was die. It felt unfair that I couldn't figure out how to do it.

In a few years I would go to therapy for the first time and learn about suicidal ideation and depression. But for the time being, it just felt like I didn't deserve anything good—I didn't deserve a future, I didn't deserve happiness, and I didn't deserve the kind of friends who would throw me a surprise birthday party.

"I'm really sorry, Alexis. I can't come. I'm sorry."

"Fine," Alexis said as she hung up abruptly.

I pressed the button and put the phone back on its cradle. I ruined parties, I ruined friendships. I ruined everything.

I rolled onto my side. Outside, a few cable company employees were laughing as they left work. Life was so easy for everyone else. I was asleep before the tears started soaking through my pillow.

I tried to cry quietly, but clearly Grandma had heard me. If she could hear this, she probably heard me all the other times, too, I thought.

My feet were already hanging over the edge of my bed; I scooted down until they hit the carpet and hoisted myself up to sitting. My T-shirt was plastered to my back with a thick sheen of sweat. It was the middle of the summer and over ninety degrees, but I had all the windows shut, trying to replicate the suffocation I felt inside on the outside.

"Child, if I have to call you down here again . . . Jesus Christ, finally," Grandma said. She was sitting on the couch, staring at me as I slouched to the chair. My chin was pulled toward my chest, my shoulders shaking with sobs.

"Dani. Look at me." She sounded as angry as she did when she caught Cory in his bedroom with his girlfriend. I looked up but couldn't see her; my eyes were puffy to the point of being almost closed. Grandma looked at me. I expected her to launch into her familiar symphony of "Get over it," but her voice was soft.

"Tell me what's wrong. No one just cries like this all the time. What is wrong—what is it? Tell Grandma."

Maybe it was the timing or the way she made her voice sound soothing and comforting, like a normal grandma.

I was exhausted.

It all came rushing out.

I didn't have a mom, well, I did, but I hated her. I hated her, because Luke used to touch me all the time and she did nothing, nothing, she made me live with him and then she ran away with him, she ran away from us for him, and I ruined your retirement because we had nowhere to go, and she didn't love me, no one loved me, and I wanted to die. I wished I was dead and I wanted to die and I couldn't figure out how to die.

A thick strand of snot was hanging from my nose, spit was pooling in the corner of my mouth, my eyes were spitting tears like a
loose fire hydrant. Everywhere, pain was leaking out of me.

Grandma interrupted. "What did you say? Did you say that
motherfucker touched you?" Her voice was shaking.

"Yes!" I let out a wail that was more like a shout. "He touched
me all the time!"

Grandma got up from the couch and came over to me. She put
her arm around my shoulder, and I pressed my face into her stomach. I thought about the snot and pulled my head away, but she
softly pressed it back into her belly.

"Okay, okay, Dani, calm down. Calm down, you hear?" Her
voice was trembling as she ran her hand up and down my back. "I
love you. You hear me? I love you."

She was crying, too, I realized.

"I love you, and your grandfather loves you. Even Cory loves
you, that numb nuts. You don't have to hurt yourself, okay? Please.
Don't hurt yourself." She released my head and put her hand under
my chin. Her voice was suddenly, shockingly firm. "I'm going to
kill him, and then I'm going to kill your mother, okay? I'm going
to kill them both, you hear me?"

I opened my eyes as far as they would go and nodded. Her
threats usually came with a smile or some indication that she was
kidding; this time, her mouth was pulled into a tense line, and she
was shaking lightly with rage. It was entirely possible in that moment for me to believe that she would actually commit murder.

"Good. Can I give you a hug?"

I nodded. Grandma got on her knees and wrapped herself around me. "It's okay. I love you."

I let myself be held in her tenderness. My sobs were fading, but she didn't stop hugging me.

We were still hugging when Bobby came downstairs with a dirty plate. "What's going on?" We looked at each other. "Were you the one screaming like that?"

"Jesus Christ, Bobby, mind your fucking business," Grandma hissed.

"I just asked a question, Ma," Bobby said loudly as he walked into the kitchen. I could hear him talking to himself as he turned on the sink.

Grandma looked at me. "You don't have to talk about this with anyone but me if you don't want to. You hear me?"

I nodded.

"Especially that pain in the ass," she said, jerking her head toward the kitchen. She leaned on the arm of the chair as she stood up. "I swear to god, I don't know what's wrong with him. So *nosy*."

I laughed, and felt it radiate through me.

I felt lighter after telling Grandma. A small amount of guilt crept in; in telling her, I just made a bad situation even worse. But for weeks after I told her, she would call me over to the couch, kiss my cheek, and tell me she loved me. I had a different sense of who Grandma was as a human being after experiencing this side of her. It was possible that I could stop assuming that no one could handle the whole mess of me and give them a chance to surprise me instead.

My depression still came back in waves, poking holes in moments that should have felt happier. But it felt less like I was carrying the weight of a secret and more that I was part of a family. Unburdening myself didn't cure me, and it would be another five years before I knew that I was suffering from depression or that I would be in a relationship with it for the rest of my life. I didn't yet know that I would take almost a dozen different antidepressants before I found the combination that worked best. I wouldn't learn to think about depression as something that occasionally happened to me as a part of my wiring, not a bomb waiting to go off all the time, until I was thirty-nine years old. And it wasn't until my forties when I learned, in therapy, how to integrate my thoughts in order to avoid sinking to the bottom of the depression well, learned how to notice warning signs and actions I could take before things got too bad. The first time I felt confident and happy again at the same time, I was forty-three years old.

Medicine and therapy were things I would discover long after I left Warwick. I wasn't cured. But seeing Grandma take care of me in the face of my terrible shame was a step toward loving each other beyond grandmother and granddaughter, as people who really understood each other.

20.

I was the first person to get my license in a house full of people who didn't drive. With no car to practice with, I mostly relied on the skills I'd used when I played *Pole Position* in the arcade while also reading the test book obsessively for a few weeks. The only time I'd been behind the wheel of a car before I took the test was when my boss's husband took me for a drive down the Palisades Parkway, right into Manhattan. The entire drive was terrifying, from the highway speeds to parallel parking in Midtown, but he was convinced that if I could survive that, I would be a great driver for the rest of my life. I borrowed their car for the actual test.

I'd had my license for about three months before Helen asked if I wanted to buy their old car. "It's just sitting here," she said one afternoon. I'd gone over to babysit and walked like I normally did. "It's a good car even if you just drive it around town."

She was referring to the 1986 navy blue Chevette parked at the end of their driveway. Maple tree branches wept leaves all over the hood and roof. It was a round little thing; some of the silver metal detail that ran down the length of the car at knee height was missing.

"You can have it for two hundred dollars and twenty hours of babysitting."

That was firmly in my price range.

I was so excited to climb behind the wheel, even though I had to hold my head as tall and straight as possible to keep the unglued ceiling cloth from draping down so far I couldn't see. Something underneath the car rumbled like a tank when I started it. I didn't care—this car was all mine.

I was driving it home for the first time when I heard a big clang. I looked back in the rearview mirror; a piece of metal the size of a sheet of loose-leaf paper had fallen out from under my car. I put it in park, ran out to grab it, and threw it in the back seat. I rounded the corner to Smith Street and swung into the parking space in front of our house.

"Is *that* the car you bought?" Grandma said. "It sounds like a goddamn army tank! Jesus, Dani—you spent your money on *that*?"

For someone who had never purchased, financed, or drove a fucking car, Grandma had a lot of opinions about them.

I had to figure out how to register and insure the car on my

own. I called the DMV and found out that Helen had to give me a
bill of sale, even if it just said that she sold it to me for a dollar.
They told me how much money to bring with me for the cost of
registration, how to get my plates, and by which date I would need
to have the car inspected. Several times over the length of the phone
call, the DMV operator asked me if I had a parent who could help
me with this. Several times, I had to say no, it was just me.

I couldn't get the car registered without insurance, so I called
the local State Farm office. Yes, I was sixteen. Yes, I would be paying for it myself. No, I could not be added to anyone else's insurance plan. Due to my age and complete lack of adult supervision in
this arena, my insurance for a two-hundred-dollar car was going
to be two thousand dollars every six months. I asked if I could
make monthly payments; they said yes. I took seven hundred dollars
out of the bank and walked it over to the insurance office the next
morning. With babysitting and my job at the convent, I thought, I
could just about afford to have a car, like everyone else.

I took a staple gun to the ceiling and tacked the cloth in place. I
had a long rectangular stencil that I picked up from Michael's;
along with a can of silver spray paint, I used it to fill in the parts of
the silver detail that were missing. I filled the back with bumper
stickers—the ubiquitous "Mean People Suck," a Bob Marley sticker,
and a host of other things that screamed "HELLO I AM A DIRT-
BAG TEENAGER PLEASE PULL ME OVER EVERY TIME I
LEAVE THE HOUSE."

When I took it in to a local mechanic for the inspection, he gave
me a list of things that needed to be fixed. "Also, your catalytic
converter is gone."

"Um, I have a part that fell off? It's in the back seat."

We both peeked in at the rusty metal part resting comfortably on the tan interior.

"Yep. That's your catalytic converter all right." The mechanic looked at me with a mix of pity and suspicion. "Look, I'll give you a replacement for it today, but you eventually have to replace the muffler, the belts, the radiator, the starter, and quite a few hoses. And that's just what we can see for now."

"Can I get it registered?" I was on a fucking mission.

"I can get ya registered if you agree to fix a few things right away. Cost you about seven hundred bucks."

That was almost all the money I had left in the bank.

"Okay."

We weren't allowed to park at school until we were seniors, so I didn't drive to school yet, but I used my car every chance I could. I drove to work, which was only a fifteen-minute walk away. I drove to pick up Alexis, and then we drove to the movies or the mall. I drove to the train station in Jersey City, so that I could take the PATH into New York City and extend my time beyond the last bus back if I needed to. I kept cassette tapes in the glove compartment and under the passenger seat, so that I was always ready for whatever mood struck, but I mostly blasted Metallica and Fugazi while I very carefully followed the speed limit on Main Street.

During the winter, my tank took on a different level of care. I was at the mechanic at least once a month now—something was always falling off, about to fall off, or making a terrible noise right before it fell off. Surely sick of having to deal with my pile of bolts every three weeks, he started giving me small tips for things I could do on my own to keep the car running, like how to tap a starter when the car wouldn't start on colder days. I kept a kit under the passenger seat that was basically a wrench and a can of starter fluid. The starter looked like a bent, inverted metal seesaw; I pushed it down on one side, sprayed the starter fluid into the crevice, and tapped on the radiator for a few seconds. The engine usually turned over after that, but I always let it run for a couple of minutes. The guys working at the cable company next door used to ask me if I needed help, but after I firmly told them no ten times in a row, they just started pointing and laughing at me every time I had the hood up.

I didn't care. I had my own car, bought with my own money, and I even knew how to fix it.

I was free.

"I'm getting a tattoo."

I had been committed to the idea of getting a tattoo ever since I saw my friend Leslie walk into class with one. It was black and red, something tribal on her shoulder. She looked tough and extremely metal. Grandma was going to California for a week to put Sweetie Pie into a nursing home, a decision she and Aunt Connie had finally made a couple of years after our visit to California, and I thought that would be the perfect time for me to announce my intentions. It was the summer before senior year; the absolute worst-case scenario would be Grandma getting so angry she wouldn't speak to me for a year, but then I would move out anyway.

"That's a stupid idea. What would you even get? It's permanent, you know. PERMANENT." Every once in a while our generational differences became crystal clear; of course she thought tattoos were silly, since she'd only ever seen them on bikers, sailors, and circus folks. It was less punk rock to her, and more of an indication that I was about to ink my way out of the workforce before I was old enough to vote.

"It's going to be delicate. I just want a needle and thread around my ankle." I knew that I was going to become a fashion designer; even if that didn't work out, I loved sewing. The permanence didn't faze me one bit.

"That's fucking ridiculous." Grandma laughed. "Do whatever you're going to do, child. It's not my body."

In my full stance as rebellious teenager, I'd never considered that she just wouldn't care. It was impossible to rebel against someone so indifferent.

Leslie drove me to her tattoo guy in Middletown. The location and visuals of the shop should have been my first indication that things were about to get a little seedier than I had originally imagined. It was a small building on the side of the freeway, across from the old mall, a Taco Bell, and a dusty florist that hadn't seen a customer since at least 1982. The large window in the front hinted to a business that was formerly happy to advertise their wares to passersby but was now covered in a black tarp. A rectangular slice was cut out of the middle, just big enough for the red neon sign that read: TATTOO. It was the perfect place to ruin your body; I was either going to get a tattoo or get murdered.

We walked in and started looking at the flash art on the wall. The stock tattoos were printed on white sheets that someone had slid into small photo books with clear plastic sleeves. I flipped through images of hearts with blank banners, crosses, and a wide assortment of skulls—with knives going through them, with flames rising out of the empty eye sockets, and, inexplicably, with blood dripping from them. Where was all that blood coming from on a bone-dry skull? I'm all for ruining my body, but let's at least make it rational.

The tribal tattoo pages were next. I don't know why they're given such a regal title as "tribal" when "jagged black lines of nonsense" would do. One looked rather pretty, though; some curved and curly lines surrounding a fleur-de-lys.

When the guy who would be inking me stepped out of the back, I flinched. He was about five-four and wearing a black tank top tucked into black jeans, which ended in square-toed black biker boots. A mix of faded and fresh tattoos traveled up his ropy, muscly arms. His curly blond mullet was impressively long in the back, reaching his midback. He wore a pair of jet-black sunglasses wrapped around his head; I couldn't see his eyes, only my own petrified reflection in the silvery mirrored lenses after I glanced down and saw that this proto Dog the Bounty Hunter type was carrying a revolver in a holster on his hip.

"Hi!" I said cheerily, eyeing the gun. "I'd like to get a tattoo."

He stared at me without responding for a solid minute. I smiled nervously and, after about thirty seconds, looked at Leslie as if to say, "Is this a good idea?" She smiled back, an old pro after her one interaction with this dude.

"You're in the right place, then," he finally said, gravel-voiced and still staring.

I didn't realize I wasn't breathing until I let out a sigh of relief. I stuck out my right leg and pointed to the floor. "Um, I want to get a needle and thread, like, wrapped around my ankle? In black?" In my nervousness, I had reverted to the kind of Valley Girl up-speak I'd abandoned years before.

He stared at me without speaking again, for longer than was comfortable. "You got a design?"

"Pardon me?" Something about the fear coursing through my veins had turned me into a turn-of-the-century southern belle catching the vapors.

"A design. I'm not gonna just free-stab on your leg."

It was the phrase "free-stab" that should have sent me running out the door without looking back, but I didn't come all the way up to Middletown just to go home without some mark of my stupidity in the face of danger permanently etched on my body.

"Oh, uh, no."

"Come back when you have a design," he garbled. "Or pick something off the wall."

I looked at Leslie, who just shrugged. How was I supposed to know that I had to bring in a drawing? And why didn't she warn me? I knew that if I left, though, I would never come back, and possibly never get a tattoo at all.

"Oh! I saw one that I liked already?" I walked to the tribal pages and flipped to the curvy fleur-de-lys one. "I could put this on my ankle? Maybe?"

The Masked Tattooist grunted, then waved a single arm to indicate that I should follow him back behind the curtain to a dentist chair with leg rests in the center of the sparse room, facing the back windows, while he rustled through a plastic bucket filled with fresh needles. I didn't expect the transaction to feel so medical, but I sat down. Leslie plopped herself into a plastic chair next to me. The tattoo guy, sunglasses still on, pressed a button on a machine that looked like the copiers in the principal's office. He pulled a pair of scissors out of a cup as the paper shot out of the tray of the machine. I'd seen enough horror movies to know that this was the part where I died, stabbed in the heart for no reason other than it would bring this maniac joy.

He started cutting the paper, put the scissors down, and sat on a tiny round stool near my leg. He grabbed a spray bottle (filled with battery acid, surely) and started spraying it on my ankle.

"What is that?!" I squeaked. I already knew that there wasn't going to be much fanfare around this particular kind of deflowering, but I thought he would at least warn me before he got to work.

He stared at me again, the spray bottle hovering over my toes. "It's water." He wiggled the piece of paper in his hand. "So I can put the design on yer ankle."

He shook his head so hard that the long part of his mullet bounced over one of his shoulders. Sunglasses still on, he affixed the paper to my ankle and slowly peeled it back. A light purple outline of the design showed faintly on my skin.

"That look about where you want it?"

I glanced at my leg quickly. "Yes," I said, with more confidence than I actually possessed.

"You have to actually look at it. Make sure it's straight. No do-overs with tattoos," he grumbled.

I was grateful for this moment of what felt like kindness, even if it was probably his wanting to avoid a lawsuit. I stared at my ankle, twisting it left and right, more enamored of the fact that this piece of skin would never be blank again than the placement of the tattoo. It looked great.

"Yes, this is very fine," I said, sounding like a farmer examining a prize cow.

He spun around on his stool, his legs under a small table, and squeezed a bottle of black ink into a tiny plastic cup. He pulled a pair of light blue plastic gloves over his nubby fingers. I tried to peek over his shoulder as he snapped rubber bands to get the tattoo gun ready. I felt confident enough to speak when he reached for the needle package.

"Is that clean?"

Having been raised in the age of AIDS, I knew that needles were a great way to transmit the disease. Even though I saw the fresh needle in the sterile package, my mind went to the most anxious place: What if he just put it in there every night to *pretend* he was using fresh needles? Like it was his own private joke how many people he was giving AIDS to without their knowing? How much did needles cost, anyway?

"You're watching me open the package. It's clean."

"Okay." My heart was pounding like a jackhammer.

"You know," he said, finally raising his sunglasses to reveal his ice-blue eyes, "I'm going to be dragging this needle around your bloody leg and I don't know anything about yer life. *You* might give *me* AIDS—ever think of that?" His lips rested into a tense line across his face as he narrowed his eyes. "How old are you, anyway?"

"I'm eighteen," I lied through my sixteen-year-old teeth. I eyed the gun again. Was it possible to annoy someone so much that they just shot you? It didn't matter; I was in the middle of trying and failing to forget the phrase "dragging this needle around your bloody leg." He could have shot me through the heart and I would have survived on the amount of adrenaline already coursing through my body.

He shook his head again and put the sunglasses down on the table. "It's a clean needle," he said again, without looking at me. For some reason, he took three paper towels off a roll, folded them into a long rectangle, and wrapped it around his fist.

I looked at Leslie. She smiled and said, "It's totally fine." I didn't believe her, but I also didn't have a choice, as the tattoo gun vibrated to life.

"Is this going to hurt?" I asked in a tone five octaves higher than my regular speaking voice.

He looked up at me, tattoo gun hovering centimeters above my ankle. "Yeah. It's definitely going to hurt." For the first time, he smiled.

My tattoo was almost healed by the time Grandma got back from California. I let her get settled for a minute before I put my foot on the couch and showed her my leg.

"I thought you were getting a needle and thread? And get your foot off my couch."

"I know," I said, putting my foot on the ground. "But then I picked this."

She squinted her eyes at my leg and leaned in to get a better look. "What is it? It's *big*."

"It's tribal. It's just . . . a design."

Grandma sat back and sighed. In my fervor to show her how cool and unique I was now, I wasn't paying attention to what she had just endured. Sweetie Pie had full dementia now. The trip couldn't have been easy. She looked exhausted.

"Well, I don't understand why you wanted to do that, but you're an adult now, I guess." She tilted her head back and closed her eyes.

I went upstairs and lay on my bed, lifting my leg up to admire the art and think about what Grandma had just said, wondering why, if I was an adult now, I felt like I had just been dismissed as if I were a child.

21.

was becoming obsessed with the notion of college. It felt like the final step of an independence I had been reaching toward for years. I fantasized about living in a dorm with no one around to make me turn off the light if I was reading past my bedtime, because I had no bedtime. My job would be to take classes and learn, which sounded like a dream come true. But more than anything, college was freedom—getting out of Warwick, surrounding myself with people who could value me in a way no one there ever could.

Aside from the year Aunt Rene spent at OCCC, no one in my immediate family had ever gone to college. Cory had no plans post–high school. Most parents were excited to think of their children fulfilling their potential, going out in the world on their own and trying to get a degree that would land them a career. Grandma thought it was a waste of time and money.

"You don't need a piece of paper to get a job, Dani."

"You do for some careers."

"Not for making clothes. I could make clothes right here," she said, gesturing around the living room.

"You don't understand," I huffed.

"I've been alive longer than you, honey—I understand more than you think."

It was the fall of senior year, and college was all anyone could think about. We were sitting around our lunch table, and I was pumping Alexis for information about how to apply. Vicki, Shimbi, and Misato were listening in. We were lunch friends; none of us really hung out outside of school. Shimbi and Misato were identical twins who had moved to Warwick from the city when we were in middle school. Misato wore heavy metal T-shirts and head-to-toe black; Shimbi was the only high schooler I'd ever known to be able to pull off a scarf without looking like someone in an Ann Taylor ad. Vicki was a boisterous Italian girl who lived in Pine Island. They were all applying to college; I was the only one who seemed to be doing it on my own, without the help of my parents, and the only one not entirely sure that going to college was a foregone conclusion.

"Shouldn't Dave be able to help with this?" Alexis knew that our guidance counselor was useless ever since he tried to dissuade her from thinking about Ivy League schools in ninth grade. I was contractually obligated to go to his office twice a year and never left feeling any more secure about my life or options.

"He thinks I should go to OCCC," I said. "Community college is all he pushes at me."

"He's a fucking asshole," Alexis said. "You're smart. You can get into a million other colleges. What are your extracurriculars?"

"My almost full-time job," I deadpanned.

Alexis rolled her eyes. "How are your grades?"

"I don't know. I failed Regents math and I hate everything except English."

"Well, just find a school that emphasizes the arts more than grades. You want to be a fashion designer, so none of that other stuff matters."

I both admired and feared Alexis's take-no-prisoners attitude toward life. Her confidence was rooted in her intelligence; she had honors classes book smarts but also a preternatural ability to figure out when adults were lying to her. She didn't suffer fools and knew she couldn't count on anyone but herself to get what she wanted in life. Instead of flowery signoffs about seeing each other in school, she simply said, "Goodbye," and hung up when she wanted to end a phone call. I would not have been surprised to find out she had a full-time job as a stockbroker on the side.

She'd also been planning her escape from Warwick for so long that I had no choice but to believe her when she said I could do it, too. Alexis was the only person in my life who told me that college was possible for me, a place where I might belong. And I believed her for two reasons: we had the same desire to get out, and her bossy mode was even more terrifying than my grandma's.

Years later, when I came home to visit from California, Alaska, Wisconsin, or England, when I had not just my bachelor's degree but my master's, I would always go to see Grandma at work. Her big smile from behind the desk at Mount Alverno instantly washed away my fears that this would be the visit when she started to resent me for leaving. Through the chorus of nuns in the lobby reciting details of my own life back to me, as told to them by Grandma, I realized that day would never come. She was proud of me, and she let everyone in her world know.

Eventually I would understand that she became uncharacteristically conservative about my going to college because she didn't have any experience there. All of her advice, both outrageous and helpful, was rooted in her ability to tell me what worked for her. How could she help me if she didn't understand the world I lived in? When I moved home for six months in order to save money for my cross-country trip to Alaska, Grandma made endless fun of me for wanting to make such a big move. One day, I saw an issue of *Alaska* magazine on the coffee table, with the telltale white address label that indicated a subscription—she was coming to terms with it by learning something about the place. Every few days, she would concede that it looked nice and that I should call her as soon as I saw my first moose.

Though maybe she simply thought college was a waste of money that she would never have and I should never borrow.

I went to the library during study hall and searched the card catalog for the big books about college that I'd seen for sale in B. Dalton at the mall. I pulled one of the huge reference tomes from the shelf and felt instantly overwhelmed. I had no idea there were so many colleges, and no idea which one was best for me. All I knew was that I wanted to make clothes for a living. Pen in hand, I started making a list on some loose-leaf paper, narrowing my choices down by program, then by state. I tried not to look at the cost.

"You'll get scholarships," Alexis said the next day at lunch. "Everyone does."

"But how do you apply?"

"You can apply to the school directly, but there are also national ones that you can use for any school."

Of course she knew about scholarships. She always figured out any information she was lacking, whether it was how to dissect a frog or how to apply to a summer soccer program in Ireland.

"But there are deadlines, so figure it out fast." She took a bite out of the lunch she made for herself every morning.

When I wasn't working, I was researching colleges. I kept a meticulous list of due dates for applications, as well as pros and cons lists for anywhere I might end up. Pro: it's in New York City. Con: if I live in the city, I might run into Mom and Luke.

I bought a book of stamps and sent letters to the ones I found interesting, asking them to mail me their catalogs and admission materials. All the stuff that showed up had white kids on the cover, but I tried not to let that psych me out. I sat at the kitchen table and filled out the applications, inevitably reaching the same stopping point for each one.

"Grandma," I called into the living room, "what's your social security number?"

"Who the fuck wants to know?" I could tell from the theme music that she was playing *Marble Madness*.

"It's for my college applications!"

"Stop yelling and come in here, for fuck's sake!"

I walked into the living room, holding one of my applications as proof. "They need your social security number and bank account stuff." She didn't look up from the game. "Because I'm a minor," I added for emphasis, "and you're my guardian."

"I'm not paying for it, so why do they need my private information?" She jerked the controller to the left as she tried to move the marble on the TV in the same direction.

"I think it's so that they can figure out how much financial aid I need?"

"All of it. Tell them you need all the financial aid they have to offer." Grandma laughed. I failed to see the humor in her being so uncooperative.

"I can't send these in without that information, Grandma."

"Well, do you have to send them this minute? I'm busy, ask me later."

A few days later, I hit up Grandma again. "I really need your social security number. I don't want to miss my deadlines."

"For what?" She was sitting on the couch, watching the news, which was as close to not busy as she was able to get.

"For my college applications!" I was about to lose my mind.

"All right! Calm down! Here, give me that," she said, gesturing to the stack of applications in my hand. "Let me look."

She lowered her glasses and looked at the tiny type over the rims. "Where do you need me to put it? I can't read any of this."

"There." I pointed.

"Here, I'll write it down on this piece of paper and you can just fill it in. Jesus."

She flipped open the Mead tablet she kept near the phone and wrote it down.

"I also need to know how much money you have in your savings account."

Grandma looked at me like I had just asked her to saw off her leg, baste it in honey, and throw it in the oven. "Are you fucking kidding me, child?"

"They want to know!" Secretly, so did I. Grandma constantly told us she didn't have money for anything, and she never missed an opportunity to tell me that she had excellent credit and no credit cards, but I really didn't have any idea where we stood financially. I knew that we weren't rich, but it was possible we were poorer than I thought.

"Just say two thousand dollars."

"Is that the truth? Because they're going to check, I think."

"Dani, I swear to god . . ."

"Okay, okay, I'll write two thousand dollars."

"Anything else?" She was peeved, staring at me over her glasses with a look that said, "There better not be anything else or I will have to end your life."

"Um, there's an application fee? It's like a hundred dollars?" I knew I was walking on thin ice here, but I had to try. Even Alexis's parents paid for her applications; most parents did.

Grandma let out a singular, rough cough. "That's why you have a job. Now get the fuck out of here."

I had a small savings account at the Bank of New York in town. Grandma didn't use checks, and I wasn't legally allowed to have any, so I withdrew some money and took the envelope to the post office to buy money orders.

"Hello," I said brightly. The employee behind the counter didn't crack a smile but looked at me expectantly. "I need five money orders. But for different amounts. The first one is for the Fashion Institute of—"

"Just tell me how much they are, and then you have to fill out the rest."

"Oh. Okay." I rattled off the application costs and grabbed the stack of money orders. I walked home and filled them out on the floor of my bedroom while watching *The Young Ones*. My applications were fanned out in front of me; I double-checked that I had all the right payments with all the right schools, put the paperwork in the envelopes they provided, and sealed them shut. Would this work? They'd probably take one look at my paltry extracurriculars and sharply declining grades and throw me right on the reject pile. I imagined that pile looked like the garbage pile from *Fraggle Rock*, except it would be the size of a mountain and on fire.

I didn't have any safety schools. I only applied for fashion design programs. There was no guarantee anyone would give me financial aid or even tell me what to do with it if I got it. All I had was a head full of desperation dressed up as hope.

The next day, I walked my applications to the post office. There was a slot on the outside of the building, but I wanted to make sure my applications were housed and protected until they were sent off. I went inside and, one by one, dropped each envelope in the Out of Town slot.

My senior year rituals revolved around the fact that I had wheels. At least three out of five days per week, I would pick up my friend Jayne at 7:00 a.m. Jayne was the third of four sisters; her dad was dead, so her mom was raising them on her own in a pretty Victorian house in town. She had a funny, deadpan sense of humor and weirdly sophisticated tastes; she lived for the J.Crew catalog and listened to Yaz.

Before I pulled out of the driveway, we'd look at each other.

"Do you feel like going today?" one of us would always ask immediately.

"No."

"Do you have any tests?"

"I have to turn in a journalism project, but I don't have that until almost last period."

"Friendly's?"

"Friendly's."

We'd watched enough teen movies to know that you never skip school in your own town; there are far too many chances to be caught. Instead, I drove us to the Friendly's in Goshen, about twenty minutes away.

After an hour or two, I'd drive us back to Jayne's house. Her older sisters were away at college, her younger sister was at school, and her mom was at work—it was the perfect place to finish our skip day once the coast was clear. Jayne usually went up to her room to sleep, and I crashed out on the couch, sometimes watching *Jerry Springer* or *The Price Is Right*. If we did go to school, we usually went around noon, when there were only two hours left in the day.

I'd spent a lifetime trying to be a good student. In the nebulous months between applying for college and waiting to hear if any school was going to accept me, I started putting my energy into feeling more like an adult instead. I was paying for almost everything in my life—my car insurance, gas, clothes. As long as I made my own money, no one could tell me what to do with it.

I didn't get into the Fashion Institute of Technology. I didn't get into most of the schools I applied to, in the end. But I did get into Lasell University, a school so small I forgot I had even applied.

Lasell was in Newton, Massachusetts, right outside of Boston down Commonwealth Avenue. I could visit New York if I got homesick, but I'd be far enough away to feel like I was free. It was an all-girls college, just like Smith, where I'd visited my friend Heather the summer before. And the fashion department was small enough that I didn't feel intimidated. It was the right move. It had to be.

Granddad called me "college girl" all summer long. He always said it with a smile, so I knew he was proud of me.

Grandma was proud of me, too, in her own way. She constantly laughed and asked me, "When are you getting the fuck out of my house again?"

Things became easier while I waited to leave. I babysat and worked at the convent all day, then spent time with friends at night. We were all going somewhere new, and were infused with the buzz of looming freedom. I went to a house party with a friend who was home for the summer, but I spent most of it in a corner reading a book about astrology. I didn't drink and found these loud idiots pretty annoying. Instead, I spent most of my time at the movies, the mall, or driving around with the windows open, watching lightning bugs glow in the trees and getting soaked by moonlight.

I knew what college was supposed to look like for kids on TV, but I didn't know what college was going to look like for me. I couldn't imagine myself going to frat parties or even getting drunk. It didn't appeal to me to think about who I might befriend or where I would live—the catalogs all showed dorm life, but what would it be like to put all my stuff into a new closet and lock the door behind me? I could only imagine the thrilling sense of independence, of being so far removed from my family that I could finally access some of the expansiveness that came with geographical distance. Warwick was almost behind me, but more importantly, everything that kept me rooted in place for so long was starting to become irrelevant. I didn't spend the summer partying and bemoaning the inevitable loss of friendship; I breathed into the possibility of who I could become more and more every day, knowing that my friends would be part of my heart forever. I was right about that—I became a godmother when Alexis gave birth to her daughter almost twenty years later; I got Christmas cards from Jayne, showcasing a new child added to the brood for a few years straight.

I took the bus to Lasell for their new-student open house, navigating my way through the Port Authority and South Station in Boston. I showed up to campus with my backpack and followed the signs to registration. Cheerful upperclassmen welcomed me and showed me to the dorms. I met Jamie, a student from Connecticut, who, by the end of the weekend, asked if I wanted to room with her. I said yes, relieved to know my roommate instead of being surprised with it upon arrival in September.

Later, Jamie would tell me that she only agreed to come to Lasell because her father promised her a car and a membership to the hunt club if she completed four years of college at any school.

"What's a hunt club?" I asked.

"Oh, it's like, for horses," Jamie said.

Lasell would end up being a horrible choice for many reasons. With no impetus to perform well at school, Jamie spent most of her time filling our room with beer cans and cheating on her boyfriend. I would become endlessly depressed during the spring semester and eventually have a complete emotional breakdown so intense three RAs were called into the room while Jamie looked on, stunned. I'd eventually get my degree many years later and many states away.

But that was all ahead of me. Everything, right then, was perfect. The future was a sparkling road with countless exit ramps, a choose-your-own-adventure book come to life.

I was given a list of things to bring with me and another list of things that were expressly forbidden, like hot pots and candles. Grandma insisted on shopping with me, and I relented. I knew I would see her at holidays; I knew I would come home. But already, I was starting to miss her.

"We'll go to Playtogs," Grandma said.

"I need nice stuff, Grandma—can we just go to Sears?"

"Playtogs is cheaper."

I rolled my eyes. "I'll just buy stuff myself."

"No," she said sternly. "My baby is going to college, and I'm allowed to buy you some things." She climbed into my car, which she hated. "It's so *small*. And *dirty*."

"I guess it's good that I'm taking it with me."

True to form, she was a back-seat driver the entire drive to Middletown. "Take the back road, not the highway," she said as we cruised into Goshen.

"I know."

"Get in that lane."

"GRANDMA. I KNOW."

By the time we got to Playtogs, I was so stressed out I wanted to leave. We walked down the aisles, looking for curtains and bedspreads.

"Would these work?" Grandma said, holding up a lacy yellow package. "What size are your windows?"

"I have absolutely no idea," I said, rolling my eyes while I pushed the cart.

"Well fuck you, then, don't have any curtains." Grandma threw the package back on the shelf.

"What about this bedspread?" The purple, turquoise, and pink pattern was more eighties than I would have liked, but I was slowly losing my will to live.

"It's great."

"Okay." She threw it in the cart. I could feel how scratchy the fabric was through the plastic bag.

"Ooooh, you're gonna need some new drawers," she said as we rounded into the aisle of underwear tubs, "in case you meet someone." I was accustomed to getting my underwear in a stocking every Christmas, a package of Hanes that served me just fine. Grandma was pinching a pair of turquoise lace bikini underwear between her thumb and forefinger.

"Gross," I said with a wince.

"What do you mean, 'gross'? Those boys you're going to be meeting won't want to do anything with you once they see those old things," she said, gesturing to my waist.

"You're the one who bought me these old things," I reminded her.

Grandma moved in close. "Do you need a new bra for your little titties?" She was cracking herself up before she even finished the question.

"Can we just *go*?"

"All right, suit yourself. You're no fun."

The week before I left, I went to the Grand Union for boxes. I was instructed by Grandma to take everything I owned aside from furniture and a box of magazines she lovingly let me keep on the balcony between my bedroom and the attic. "Once you leave, that's *my* room," she said. Most kids got four years before their parents started reclaiming space; I got four weeks.

The guy at the deli counter brought a stack out of the back, neatly folded and resting under his arm.

"Thank you," I said, smiling. "I'm packing for college."

"Oh yeah? Good for you." He turned around to snap on some gloves and get back to work.

———

Grandma has dementia now. On her bad days, she can't remember what happened from one minute to the next. On her good days, she leaves her appointments at the hospital loudly telling all the doctors and nurses that they are assholes for making her wait for an elevator or for doing any of the scheduled exams, punctuated by her Pillsbury Doughboy laugh. She is still herself, even in the face of a disease that threatens to erase her completely. She still knows my voice and my face, though I know the day is coming when she will not recognize either.

My granddad has been dead for almost twenty years; his lung cancer progressed quickly, and he was gone before my plane landed, before I had the chance to say goodbye. They were not one of those couples you read about on Upworthy, the ones who couldn't live without each other, one spouse passing the week after their beloved died; she misses him, but Grandma outlived Granddad mostly out of spite. She keeps his ashes on a shelf in her bedroom behind her *Saw* and *Hostel* DVDs and says "good morning" and "goodnight" to him every day. During one visit, I called the office of her retirement community to insist that they give her a cutout for a walk-in shower immediately, while I was there, to ensure it was done properly. Grandma beamed at me while I scowled at the phone. "You always know how to get things done. Just like your grandma."

Since she insists on her independence, I hired a nurse for Grandma once it was clear that she needed help navigating, remembering to eat, remembering to take her medication. She constantly tells me that I shouldn't waste the money, that she's fine on her own. When I remind her that I'm a television writer now, she sucks in her breath and says, "Oh my GOD, Dani. Never mind—you're a rich bitch." I'm not, but I can afford to take care of us both, and that's more than I ever thought I would be able to do.

She *is* okay on her own sometimes.

She's still herself.

But when she wakes up every morning, she cries for her mother and grandmother, both long gone, leaning on the kitchen counter for stability while her coffee simmers, her tears soaking the neck of her shirt. "I want my mommy," she wails in her confusion. On my last visit, when I camped out with her after her cataract surgery, I put framed pictures of Sweetie Pie and my great-great-grandmother on Grandma's nightstand, hoping they would soothe her. She wants her mommy, but she has me instead.

She'll never remember what I tell her now—that this is what makes me proud of who I am, proud of what I've been through, to get to this place where I can take care of her. Our relationship has flipped, but my family has never been good at sticking with traditional roles. We became each other's lifelines, Grandma and me. When I was born and the nurse held me like a football, when I opened my creepy little eyes, the first person I saw was my grand-mother. I opened my eyes and saw the love of my life.

When her dementia feels too heavy to carry, when I look at pictures and remember her when she was whole, when I wonder how I survived and how I escaped, I think about the morning Grandma sent me off to college.

When it was time for me to leave, my car was packed with so much stuff the back was five inches lower than usual. It was a bright morning. Grandma was standing on the porch, watching me shove a garbage bag full of clothes into the hatchback. I slammed the trunk closed.

"You have your maps? You know where you're going?" She stood with her arms crossed while I reached into the passenger seat through the window to show her my atlas.

"I've got it."

"Do you have *everything* you need?"

I looked at the bulging car. "You made me take everything I own, so yeah, I *genuinely* have everything I need."

"Come here." I walked up the steps. Grandma reached up and grabbed my face in her hands. "You call me the minute you get there, you hear me?"

"Yes, Grandma," I said through squished cheeks.

"I love you so much." She kissed my forehead, then kissed each cheek.

I gave her a hug, holding on for a little longer than I usually did. She pushed me away. "Who loves you?"

"You do, Grandma," I said, rolling my eyes.

"Okay, get going. You don't want to be on the road after dark."

I bounded down the steps, into my car, into my future. I clicked the seat belt into place and looked up through the windshield. Grandma blew me a kiss and waved, and I waved back.

I was too excited to cry as I backed out of the driveway. No matter what happened next, I had made the first step. I had momentum.

I put the car in drive and waved at Grandma one last time. I leaned over the seat and rolled down the passenger window. "I'll see you at Thanksgiving!" I shouted.

"Keep your eyes on the goddamn road!" Grandma shouted back.

I turned onto Main Street, taking the familiar fork at the Mobil and veering toward Middletown. Instead of pulling off at the mall exit like usual, I kept going.

I kept going.

Acknowledgments

My friend and agent, Christopher Schelling. You are a man of astounding taste, impeccable style, and unlimited patience, but I love your horrible taste in television most of all. Thank you for every Connecticut weekend, for your unending fight to get this book in the right hands, for talking me down from the ledge, and pushing me to connect to the part of myself that could do this work.

My editors, Andrea Schulz and Emily Wunderlich, the most gifted people on planet Earth. Thank you for your patience through all 375 years it took me to write this book. There's not a single page that wasn't made infinitely better by your intelligence and humor. You got it, from the very beginning, and I am endlessly grateful to know you both.

Augusten Burroughs, without whom this book would not exist.

Thank you for the myriad ways you told me to just *write* it, for responding enthusiastically to my childhood stories around the dinner table, for infusing me with hope in the beautiful example of your wild life, for the stunning depths of your friendship. There is no one else with whom I would rather watch four hours of Whitney Houston videos.

My TV team: Lindsay Perraud, Laura Gordon, Robby Koch, Belva Anakwanze, and Jonathan Drubner. Thank you for making sure I get paid like a white man, and for believing in my talent when I absolutely did not.

Marie Andreakos, Amelia Gray, Caroline Williams, Ann Friedman, Jason Butler Harner, Rebecca Woolf, Corina Maritescu, Laura Krafft, Ramou Sarr, Eden Kennedy, Emily Tyra, Adam Santucci, Isabelle Dimang, Patrick Somerville, Neal Brennan, Steven Avalos, Nick and Faryl Amadeus, and Dan Steinbacher: I will never forgive you for your tremendous efforts at making Los Angeles somewhat bearable and fun for me. I'm absolutely disgusted that I like it here so much, and you are all 100 percent to blame.

Reyhan Harmanci, Patrick Hoffman, Jason Schwartz, Tavi Gevinson, Jennifer Abbots, Marlena Bittner, Maggie Serota, Alexis Coe, Julie Klausner, Estelle Tang, Taffy Akner, Lourdes Uribe, Heather Hall, Bekah Havens, Alison Benson, Nick Hughes, Kurt Schlachter, and Emma Straub: Don't read that part about how much I like Los Angeles. We know where my true heart belongs—in New York City, buried somewhere in a sidewalk trash heap crawling with rats on a beautiful, hot summer day. Here's to getting drunk in Queens and waking up in Brooklyn, to adding another chair at Café Loup, to coffee at Buvette that turns into dinner, to bookstores, to dancing, to Mets games, to the 2/3, to costumes pulled out of the middle of the street, to half of Manhattan, to all of Harlem.

Deneen Vines, Chandler Stanley, Ben Wright, Diane Pell, and Helen, Ryan, Jeremy, Jansen, and C. J. Truitt: Thank you for always giving me a soft place to land, then and now. Ryan Scafuro, Brendan McManus, Garrett Talbot, Timothy Hull, Amy Baglione, and Jayne Fruh, for helping me see the good side of that little farm town that raised us.

Tally Abecassis, Amy Elz, Kelly Sue DeConnick, Susie Gharemani, Taryn Mazza, Monica Heisey, Antonia Cornwell, Jessica Hopper, Maile Knight: a greater support system has never existed. Thank you for the Emotional Voltron that is your continued love, intelligence, and humor.

Millie DeChirico, my friend, my business partner, and my consigliere. You are a little secret knife come to life, and mine would be infinitely worse without you.

Thandie Newton, my dearest sis, for your epic generosity, strength, and persistence. I'm grateful for the very miracle of you.

Rainbow Rowell, thank you for fielding the tears, for creating so much of the laughter. I'm down for an entire meal served on a garbage can lid, anytime.

Dr. Donna Gable, I am eternally grateful for all the ways you put me on this path to healing, and continue to be my guide.

Dr. Elizabeth Richards, thank you for reminding me that while I am a person who experiences depression, that does not mean it is a bomb waiting to blow up inside of me. I would not have started this book without your support.

Lorraine Redmon—for being part of Team Dementia, and helping me care for my grandma from so far away. I don't know what we would do without you.

Sarah Brown, why aren't we buying cheap cocktail rings at Accessorize *right now*? You are every support beam of the shaky span bridge that is my life, and without you I would crumble. Thank you for your grace, your wisdom, and your heart. In the words of a true hero . . . Moooobb Deep Eep Meep Beep Creep Seep Leep, always.

Sarah Jackson, for the "Fuck! Everything!" energy you've carried from the halls of Warwick Valley High School to now. I hope we still call each other at 3:00 a.m. when we are covered in gray hair. Yours is the voice I hear in my head whenever I am starting something new, the laugh whenever I do something ridiculous. Thank you for all of these lessons over all of these years.

Sandra Pieloch, the scaffolding of my heart. Every adventure, in every state, on every continent has been guided by the expansiveness of your spirit. Thank you for building your life on love, for making all the hard decisions first so I had a map to follow, for being my family.

Alexis Larkin: the Jerry Sizzler to my Jerry Sizzler. Thank you for every last second of the past thirty years, for being front and center in all my best memories. Thank you for bringing Valentina into my life. I promise to ask for your permission before I take her to get her first tattoo.

Aunt Connie—your grace and eloquence are surpassed only by your capacity to love. Thank you for telling me to keep a journal all those decades ago, and for teaching me how to sneak into the movies.

Aunt Rene, thank you for teaching me how to break free, and, in your final selfless act, for showing me how to forgive.

Mom. For the fresh start, and all the years in between.

Cory—thank you for surviving all of this with me, for phone calls where all I can do is cry, for always knowing what to say. Janet, thank you for loving him, and us.

Grandma—you are a maniac, the *worst* advice giver, the funniest person I've ever met, and the love of my life. Thank you for saving me. Thank you for teaching me how to save myself.